MATT AND TOM O

ULTIMATE
FOOTBALL HEROES

POGBA

FROM THE PLAYGROUND
TO THE PITCH

DINO

The

Published by Dino Books
an imprint of John Blake Publishing
3 Bramber Court, 2 Bramber Road,
London W14 9PB, England

www.johnblakebooks.com

www.facebook.com/johnblakebooks ▋
twitter.com/jblakebooks ▋

First published in paperback in 2017
This edition published in 2018

ISBN: 978 1 78606 929 0

British Library Cataloguing-in-Publication Data:

A catalogue record for this book is available from the British Library.

Design by www.envydesign.co.uk

Printed and bound in Great Britain by Clays Ltd, St Ives plc

1 3 5 7 9 10 8 6 4 2

Papers used by John Blake Publishing are natural, recyclable products made from
wood grown in sustainable forests. The manufacturing processes conform to the
environmental regulations of the country of origin.

Every attempt has been made to contact the relevant copyright-holders, but some
were unobtainable. We would be grateful if the appropriate people could contact us.

John Blake Publishing is an imprint of Bonnier Publishing
www.bonnierpublishing.co.uk

For Noah and the future Oldfields to come
Looking forward to reading this book together

ULTIMATE
FOOTBALL HEROES

Matt Oldfield is an accomplished writer and the editor-in-chief of football review site *Of Pitch & Page*. Tom Oldfield is a freelance sports writer and the author of biographies on Cristiano Ronaldo, Arsène Wenger and Rafael Nadal.

Cover illustration by Dan Leydon.
To learn more about Dan visit danleydon.com
To purchase his artwork visit etsy.com/shop/footynews
Or just follow him on Twitter @danleydon

TABLE OF CONTENTS

ACKNOWLEDGEMENTS 7

CHAPTER 1 – **POGBACK** 9

CHAPTER 2 – **RENARDIÈRE** 15

CHAPTER 3 – **THE POG FAMILY** 21

CHAPTER 4 – **WORLD CUP '98** 27

CHAPTER 5 – **US ROISSY** 32

CHAPTER 6 – **EURO 2000** 38

CHAPTER 7 – **FOOTBALL MAD** 43

CHAPTER 8 – **US TORCY** 50

CHAPTER 9 – **LE HAVRE** 55

CHAPTER 10 – **CAPTAIN OF FRANCE** 61

CHAPTER 11 – **MOVING TO MANCHESTER** 67

CHAPTER 12 – **TOP DOG** 74

CHAPTER 13 – **LEARNING FROM LEGENDS** 83

CHAPTER 14 – **FIRST-TEAM FRUSTRATIONS** 89

CHAPTER 15 – **POGBOOM** 96

CHAPTER 16 – **FUTURE OF FRANCE** 103

CHAPTER 17 – **GOLDEN BOY** 110

CHAPTER 18 – **GOALDEN BOY** 118

CHAPTER 19 – **WORLD CUP 2014** 124

CHAPTER 20 – **CHALLENGING FOR THE CHAMPIONS
LEAGUE AGAIN** 130

CHAPTER 21 – **THE DAB** 138

CHAPTER 22 – **EURO 2016** 144

CHAPTER 23 – **REUNITED** 152

ACKNOWLEDGEMENTS

First of all, I'd like to thank John Blake Publishing – and particularly my editor James Hodgkinson – for giving me the opportunity to work on these books and for supporting me throughout. Writing stories for the next generation of football fans is both an honour and a pleasure.

I wouldn't be doing this if it wasn't for Tom. I owe him so much and I'm very grateful for his belief in me as an author. I feel like Robin setting out on a solo career after a great partnership with Batman. I hope I do him (Tom, not Batman) justice with these new books.

Next up, I want to thank my friends for keeping

me sane during long hours in front of the laptop.
Pang, Will, Mills, Doug, John, Charlie – the laughs
and the cups of coffee are always appreciated.

I've already thanked my brother but I'm also very
grateful to the rest of my family, especially Melissa,
Noah and of course Mum and Dad. To my parents, I
owe my biggest passions: football and books. They're
a real inspiration for everything I do.

Finally, I couldn't have done this without Iona's
encouragement and understanding during long,
work-filled weekends. Much love to you.

CHAPTER 1

POGBACK

'This is a must-win match,' José Mourinho told his Manchester United team before their home game against Premier League champions Leicester City. 'Today, we need our leaders to lead.'

Paul knew that he was one of the leaders that Mourinho was talking about. His £89 million return to Old Trafford had been the biggest transfer story of summer 2016. The '#PogBack' campaign had taken over the Twittersphere and thousands of fans bought his '6 POGBA' shirt and copied his cool tricks and hairstyles.

After moving to play for Juventus at the age of eighteen, four years later Paul was back at

Manchester United. The French player had established himself as an international superstar and a four-time Italian league winner. Expectations were very high. Ever since Paul Scholes's retirement, United had been seeking a match-winning midfielder and Paul fitted the bill: a box-to-box midfielder who could tackle, dribble and shoot. He was part-Patrick Vieira, part-Zinedine Zidane and part-Ronaldinho, and he would bring glory days back to Old Trafford. That was Mourinho's big plan when he took over as manager.

But after a great start to the new season against Southampton, United had lost two matches in a row to local rivals Manchester City and then to Watford. Lots of people were already criticising Paul. Was he really as good as people said he was? Why wasn't he controlling games? Why hadn't he scored any goals? Why had United paid so much money for him?

'Don't listen to the negative comments,' his mum, Yeo, told him. She was a very important part of Paul's life, offering advice and support when he needed it most. 'We all know how good you are!'

English football was much faster and more physical

than Italian football. Paul needed time to adapt, to gel with his new teammates and to rediscover his form. But he didn't have time. The Manchester United fans were impatient for success.

'We've spent lots of money on great new players,' they argued. 'We have to win the league this season!'

'It's time to shine,' Paul said to himself as he walked out of the tunnel and onto to the Old Trafford pitch. The noise of the crowd only added to his adrenaline. With 70,000 fans cheering his name, it really was the Theatre of Dreams. Paul was a cool character and he never felt nervous, even when the pressure was on. He believed in his own talent and he was determined to win. Today, his usual dyed blond hair was gone; Paul meant business.

From the kick-off, he pushed the team forward with his quick passing and powerful runs. United took the lead through a Chris Smalling header and it gave them the confidence to keep attacking. Leicester just could not cope with the pace and trickery of Jesse Lingard, Marcus Rashford, and especially Paul. He was running the show.

As he dribbled forward, he chipped an amazing pass through to Zlatan Ibrahimović, who chested the ball down and volleyed just over the bar.

'That would have been the best goal ever!' Paul said with a big smile on his face. He was really enjoying himself.

When Paul got the ball on the left, he only had one thought: shoot. He cut inside and hit a rocket of a shot. *Booooooooooom!* The ball swerved through the air. The goalkeeper had no chance but it struck the post.

'Nearly!' Paul said to himself. 'Next time, I'll score.'

Juan Mata dribbled forward and passed to Paul. Without taking a touch to control the ball, he flicked a beautiful pass to Jesse, who flicked the ball into Juan's path. Juan fired into the net to complete a great team goal.

'What an unbelievable move!' Marcus shouted as they all celebrated together.

United's team were on fire and three minutes later, Marcus made it 3-0. Then just before half-time, Daley Blind swung a corner into the penalty area.

Paul used his strength and height to get past his marker and head the ball into the far corner.

Goooooooooooooooooooooaaaaaaaaaaaaaaaaaaaaaaa llllllllllllllllllllllllllllllllll!!!!!!

Paul finally had his first Manchester United goal and it was an amazing feeling. The supporters expected to see his trademark celebration, 'The Dab', but they would be disappointed. Instead, Paul pointed towards the sky and breathed a sigh of relief. He was finally off the mark, four years after making his club debut, and he was starting to prove his critics wrong.

'Congratulations, that will be the first of many!' Jesse said, giving his friend a big hug.

It was the kind of man-of-the-match performance that Mourinho had broken the world transfer record for. Each time Paul got the ball, every touch was positive and exciting, and the Manchester United fans cheered loudly and hoped for another goal. He was the heart of the team, just as Mourinho had told him to be.

'That's much better!' the manager told him at the

final whistle. 'You're a world-class player and you showed that today.'

Paul was pleased with his display and, most importantly, with the three points from the win. He had returned to Old Trafford dreaming of winning the biggest trophies: the Premier League, the FA Cup and the Champions League. Every victory was a step towards achieving those goals.

'Yes, but I can do even better,' Paul replied, full of confidence.

He was always looking to improve. He had learnt from the best – Patrick Vieira, Zinedine Zidane, Paul Scholes and Andrea Pirlo – and he was still learning from the best. Superstars like Zlatan and Wayne Rooney had lots of experience and tips to share. Paul was ready to do everything possible to be the best midfielder in the world.

He had come a long way from the Renardière estate in France but he was still the same Paul he had always been. He was curious, competitive, gifted, unique, but above all, a born leader and a born winner.

CHAPTER 2

RENARDIÈRE

'I want to play!' Paul shouted, tugging on Mathias's shirt. 'Let me play! It's my turn!'

He had been watching his twin brothers playing table tennis for hours and he was really bored. It was raining heavily and he hated staying inside. There was nothing fun for him to do. He wanted to be running around on the grass in the middle of the estate but his brothers were happy to stay dry in their big white tower block.

Mathias ignored him and so Paul stamped his foot and tugged Florentin's shirt instead. When they went out to play, the twins had to look after their younger brother. Paul was only three years old, two years younger than them, but he wanted to do everything that they did. He followed them everywhere, like a shadow.

'Okay fine, this should be funny,' Florentin said, handing him a bat. 'It's about as big as your whole arm!'

Mathias hit the serve and the ball flew straight past Paul. He barely even saw it. With his second shot, Mathias hit the ball even harder. This time, Paul saw it but there was no way that he could react quickly enough.

'Come on, go easy on him!' Florentin laughed. 'He's only a baby! You've got to give him a chance.'

This time, the ball moved much more slowly and Paul focused hard and hit the ball back over the net. It bounced right on the edge and fell to the floor before Mathias could reach it. Paul had won the point – and his brother wasn't happy.

'What a lucky shot! Where did you learn to do that?' Mathias asked.

Paul shrugged – he had been watching his brothers for ages! As it got darker and darker outside, he got better and better indoors at table tennis. He was determined to show off in front of his older brothers and it helped that he was a natural at all sports. Mathias and Florentin were relieved when they heard their mother Yeo calling from upstairs.

'Boys, it's time to come home now!'

If they were playing football with the other local kids, Yeo usually had to shout six or seven times before her sons came home. 'It was last goal wins!' was their usual excuse as they washed their hands quickly before sitting down for dinner. But today, without football, they came straight away. She heard their little feet tapping up the many steps that led to their apartment.

Residence La Renardière in Roissy-en-Brie wasn't the best place to live but it certainly wasn't the worst. Yeo was very grateful to have a good community around her. Most of the families in Renardière had come to France from African countries like Guinea, Senegal or Mali, and they loved to share their music, dancing and cooking. Mathias, Florentin and Paul had lots of friends to play with and as long they were together and nearby, Yeo knew that they were safe.

'Hi Mum, what's for dinner?' Mathias asked as he ran through the door and jumped on to the sofa. Suddenly, the small flat was full of noise and movement once again, although Yeo preferred it when they had been playing football because they always returned quiet and exhausted.

'Chicken, rice and beans,' she replied. Even though she worked very hard, Yeo always tried to make sure that her growing boys had a good, healthy diet.

'Urghhh, not again!' Florentin shouted but Yeo was too busy putting the food on the plates to listen to him.

'What have you been up to today?' she asked when they sat down to eat.

'We played table tennis and I won!' Paul boasted happily.

'No you didn't!' the twins shouted together. Florentin gave his younger brother a little slap around the head.

'Well, nearly,' Paul replied, with the cheeky smile that Yeo loved.

'At least they are letting him join in,' she thought to herself as she filled their plates with seconds.

'I hope it doesn't rain again tomorrow,' Mathias said with his mouth full. 'We need to carry on that football match – my team is so much better than yours!'

Florentin wasn't so sure about that. 'No way, we're only two goals behind – we're going to win!'

This is how it was every night in the Pogba household but the arguments were always friendly. Yeo was so glad that her sons didn't fight with each other.

'Can I play with you tomorrow?' Paul asked, and his brothers fell silent. Every week he asked and every week they said no. He was still too young and small to play with the big boys but he was also too good for the younger boys. He could already kick the ball really hard and it wasn't that much fun dribbling around players all day long. He wanted a challenge.

'When you turn four, I promise you can play with us,' Florentin said.

'You won't like it. You'll get hurt and you'll cry,' Mathias added but Paul glared at him. He wasn't in the mood for nasty jokes. He was strong enough to play and brave enough to cut his knees and carry on.

'Would anyone like ice cream?' Yeo asked and suddenly everything was fine again.

She knew exactly how to get her sons to behave. They were good boys but sometimes she had to be strict with them. She wanted them to learn right from wrong, so that they didn't get into trouble when they became teenagers.

'Now, whose turn is it to help me wash the dishes?'

Mathias pointed at Paul, who pointed at Florentin, who pointed at Mathias. Yeo laughed. 'Well, I guess we'll all do it together then!'

CHAPTER 3

THE POG FAMILY

As he watched the football match from the sidelines, Antoine couldn't help smiling. He had seen Mathias and Florentin play many times before at Renardière but this was the first time that he had seen his youngest son in action too. Little Paul was still only four years old but he was fighting hard against the older kids. His brothers weren't protecting him now but with the ball at his feet, he looked comfortable. His technique was very good for someone so young. There was a lot of potential.

'He's going to be even better than the twins!' Antoine thought to himself proudly.

Back in Guinea, Antoine had been a very good

footballer but when he moved to France at the age of thirty, it was much harder to find a good team. He carried on playing because he loved the game but as he got older, he became more and more affected by injury. By the time his sons were born, his own career had faded but he was determined that his sons would fare better.

'You'll be the football heroes that I also wanted to be,' he told them.

Antoine and Yeo had separated when Paul was only two years old but he still lived nearby. Whenever the boys stayed with him at weekends, he took them to Paris Saint-Germain matches and they watched other games on TV too, especially when Paul's favourite team Marseille were in action.

Antoine always encouraged his sons to watch carefully. 'Did you see that piece of skill?' he would say, pointing at the screen. If it was on video, he would rewind to show it again. 'To be the best, you have to keep learning new things. You must never be lazy!'

When the match ended, Paul went over to see his dad.

'Well played out there, kid!' Antoine said, giving him a big hug.

Paul had a few cuts on his legs but he had the biggest smile on his face. 'They might be bigger but I'm more skilful,' he told his dad proudly.

Antoine nodded – confidence was very important. 'What you need to learn next is how to look up and play great passes,' he said. 'Dribbling is fun but it's not always the best thing to do. Sometimes, you need to see where your teammates are. It's a team game.'

Paul listened carefully – he wanted to improve and his dad knew lots about football. But he was still very young and he really loved dribbling and doing skills. It looked much cooler than passing, even if sometimes it got him in trouble. The bigger boys didn't like being embarrassed by a kid two years younger than them and often they kicked his ankles or pushed him to the ground. Sometimes Paul went home crying but he always came back the next day to play another football match. He needed to be tough to become a superstar.

Every time Antoine watched Paul play, he gave him new tips. Sometimes, if Paul was joking around with his friends or he wasn't running enough, Antoine would shout 'Focus!' and suddenly Paul would sprint to win the ball. With his dad's help, he was getting better and better.

But one day, Paul saw his dad coaching some of the boys on the other team. He was really confused.

'Why are you helping Mamadou?' Paul asked. 'You should be helping me!'

Antoine laughed. 'I *am* helping you! If you want to be the best, you need to play against the best opponents. It's too easy for you at the moment, so I'm trying to give you more of a challenge.'

Pitted against Mamadou, Paul struggled for a while to get away from his defender. His opponent was following him everywhere on the pitch and he was ready for all of Paul's tricks. Paul couldn't find the space that he needed to score a goal, and when he lost the ball, his teammates weren't happy.

'Pass the ball!'

'Stop showing off!'

Paul was getting more and more frustrated and he looked to his dad for help. But Antoine stayed silent – he wanted his youngest son to work it out for himself.

The next time he got the ball, Paul took one touch, played a short pass and ran further up the pitch. It caught Mamadou by surprise and he couldn't keep up. When he got the ball back, Paul had found that space he needed. But instead of shooting or dribbling, he looked for his teammates again. He was really thinking about the game now. Moussa made a great run from the left wing and Paul played a perfect pass behind the defence for his teammate to score. His mistakes were quickly forgotten as they celebrated a brilliant goal.

On the sideline, Antoine clapped and smiled. 'He's learning quickly!' he said to himself.

Mathias and Florentin were faster and stronger but they always wanted their little brother on their team. Florentin at the back, Paul in midfield and Mathias in attack – it was an incredible line-up. 'You think you can beat the "Pogfamily"?' they would joke before the game started but no-one could. They were unbeatable. They all had nicknames: their mum was 'Mamso', Mathias was 'Le Dos' ('The Back'), Florentin was 'Le Zerr', and Paul was 'La Pioche', which meant 'The Pickaxe'.

'It's because you're always helping the team, rather than playing for yourself,' Florentin explained to him. Paul loved the name. Sometimes they had arguments but Paul loved competing with this brothers.

'One day, we'll all be professional footballers,' Paul told them, 'and we'll play for the same team. Think how many trophies we can win!'

CHAPTER 4

WORLD CUP '98

It was all anyone was talking about in Renardière, and everywhere else across the country too. Could France really beat Brazil to win the World Cup Final? After winning their group and then beating Paraguay, Italy and Croatia, they were now one step away from glory. 'Les Bleus' had never won the World Cup before but this was their best opportunity to do it.

'We've got Youri Djorkaeff and Zinedine Zidane,' Mathias argued. 'With their skills, we could beat anyone!'

'But Brazil have got Ronaldo,' Florentin replied. 'He's the best player in the world. Rivaldo sets him up and he scores goals for fun!'

'Yes, but our defence is brilliant,' Mathias said, counting the stars on his fingers. 'Fabien Barthez, Lilian Thuram, Bixente Lizarazu, Laurent Blanc and Marcel Desailly. We've only conceded two goals in six matches so far. We can definitely stop Ronaldo and Rivaldo.'

Paul didn't know the players as well as his brothers did but he loved watching football. It was a very exciting time in France. Not only was the tournament taking place on home soil but the national team were doing really well. There were lots of new heroes and many of them had roots in African countries, just like the Pogba brothers. Marcel Desailly was born in Ghana, Patrick Vieira was born in Senegal, and Zidane's parents came from Algeria.

'That could be us in twelve years, playing for France at World Cup 2010!' Paul suggested as he sat down to watch the final on TV with his brothers. The five-year-old would still only be seventeen years old by then but he really believed it could happen.

Paul had goosebumps as he watched the players run out on to the pitch at the Stade de France, only one hour's train journey away from where they lived. Two-thirds of the stadium was coloured blue and red for France and one-third was green and yellow for Brazil.

'Imagine how good the atmosphere must be,' Mathias said. 'I wish we could be there.'

After the national anthems, it was time for kick-off. 'Come on France!' the Pogba brothers shouted.

From the first minute, Zidane was the best player on the pitch. The Juventus playmaker was magical and Paul couldn't take his eyes off him. He loved the way Zidane always knew what to do next: when to run with the ball and when to play a clever pass instead. And he always looked so calm, as if he had all the time in the world.

'We need to get a goal!' Florentin said. He looked very nervous as Stéphane Guivarc'h missed a good chance. 'What's wrong with Ronaldo? He doesn't look dangerous at all.'

Halfway through the first half, Petit took a corner for France. Zidane made a great late run into the box and headed the ball powerfully into the bottom corner. The Stade de France went wild and so did the Pogba living room.

'What a goal!'

'Zizou is amazing!'

'He can do everything!'

As the first half was coming to an end, France won another corner. Djorkaeff crossed the ball and Zidane headed it straight past the goalkeeper and into the net. 2-0 to France!

'He's done it again!' Paul shouted and he lifted his shirt over his head in celebration.

'Brazil can't come back from that – we're about to win the World Cup!' Florentin told them with a massive grin on his face and he was right. In the last minute of the match, Petit scored to make it 3-0. It was party time in France. At the final whistle, the Pogba brothers hugged just like the players on the pitch.

Campeones! Campeones! Olé! Olé! Olé!

'That's the best game I've ever seen!' Paul said as the players walked up to collect their medals and the famous gold World Cup trophy. He would never forget the final, and especially Zidane's man-of-the-match-performance. For ninety minutes, he was everywhere on the pitch – tackling in defence, running forward with the ball, creating chances and scoring goals.

Zizou was the complete midfielder, and exactly the kind of player that Paul wanted to become. He wanted to be a legend and play in all of the biggest finals and win all of the biggest trophies. Zidane and his France teammates were the inspiration that Paul needed to work even harder. One day, he wanted to inspire the next generation of French kids. That was the big aim.

'I can't wait to play football tomorrow!' he told his brothers, as they ran out into the street to share their joy with the rest of Renardière.

CHAPTER 5

US ROISSY

'I think you're ready,' Antoine said as he picked Paul
up after another game at Renardière. Paul's team had
thrashed their opponents and he was at the centre
of everything. It looked so easy for him. 'Too easy,'
Antoine thought to himself.

'Ready for what?' Paul asked.

'Ready for US Roissy!' Antoine replied and Paul
punched the air with joy.

From the top of the tower block where they lived,
Paul could see the Stade Paul Bessuard, home of
US Roissy-en-Brie. It wasn't the Stade de France but
it had a big pitch with perfect grass and a stand for
supporters, and it was only a five-minute walk away.

Mathias and Florentin already played for the club and Paul had been waiting impatiently to join his brothers there. Competitive eleven-a-side football was the new challenge that he needed as he looked to develop his skills.

'Great, how soon can I start?' Paul asked impatiently.

'Next week!' his dad said.

'Welcome to US Roissy,' Aziz Keftouna said, shaking Paul's hand and giving him one of the club's red shirts. The youth coach looked very friendly but Mathias and Florentin had told him all about the strict rules at the club. Paul would have to behave well and show respect for everyone. It was time to get serious about football.

Keftouna liked what he saw as Paul warmed up with his new teammates. He was taller than most of the other boys and he was very quick, with two good feet.

'He's got the right skills but does he have the right attitude?' Keftouna thought to himself. There were lots of very talented kids in the local area but many of them didn't want to work hard to improve. They thought they were already good enough and didn't like it when Keftouna shouted at them to do more. He only wanted hard workers in his team.

Keftouna had coached Paul's brothers in the past and so he knew that the Pogbas were a very gifted and competitive family. Their dad, Antoine, had taught them to strive to be the best and he was watching Paul's debut from the side of the pitch. There would be no messing about.

In the practice match at the end of training, Paul's long legs never stopped moving. He was determined to impress his new coach. Whenever his team lost the ball, he chased and chased until he won it back. He was as hungry as a wolf and his opponents were scared. When his team had possession, he ran into space and called for the ball. With the ball at his feet, Paul slowed down and thought hard. 'What would Zizou do?' he always said to himself. Instead of trying to score an amazing goal, he looked for the killer pass instead. Keftouna had never seen such a mature six-year-old footballer.

'Well played!' he said, giving Paul a big pat on the back. 'That was an incredible performance today. But can you do that every match?'

Paul nodded confidently – there was no doubt about that.

Keftouna saw that Paul was already getting on really well with the other boys. As soon as training ended, he was joking around, singing and doing silly dances. They were all laughing together as if they had been friends for years.

'What do you think of Paul?' Keftouna asked his captain, Abdel, as they left the stadium.

'He's brilliant and he's really funny too,' Abdel replied. 'With him in midfield, we can win the league!'

Keftouna had a very good feeling about his new player. With the right kind of discipline and encouragement, Paul got better and better. At the centre of the pitch, he controlled games and helped US Roissy to win game after game. Paul was a very skilful player but he also worked hard for the team.

It was all going very well but Keftouna liked to challenge his youngsters.

'Paul, I want you to do 150 keepy-uppies in a row,' he said at the end of one training session a few months later.

'Easy!' Paul replied straight away. He spent hours every day practising his tricks. How hard could it be?

'It has to be fifty with your right foot, then fifty with your left foot, and finally fifty with your head. Do you still think that's easy?'

Keftouna could see the fire in Paul's eyes – he would do everything to succeed. But when the boy failed to turn up for the next two days of training, the coach got worried. Had he pushed his player too hard?

'Has anyone seen Paul?' Keftouna asked his team but everyone shook their heads.

On the third day, Paul was back with a ball under his arm and a big smile on his face. 'Coach, I'm ready for the challenge!' he shouted.

His teammates formed a circle around him and started to count.

1, 2, 3... 25, 26, 27... 48, 49, 50!!

Without stopping, Paul switched the ball on to his left foot.

1, 2, 3... 25, 26, 27... 48, 49, 50!!

With the fiftieth, Paul skilfully flicked the ball up and began his headers.

1, 2, 3... 25, 26, 27...

He was making it look really easy. It was like the ball was stuck to his head. His teammates were counting louder and louder.

40, 41, 42, 43, 44, 45, 46, 47, 48, 49, 50!!!!!!!!!!!!!!

As he finished, Paul shrugged and flicked the ball over his head. 'Easy!' he said as his teammates jumped on him to celebrate.

'I'll need to come up with some more challenges for you,' Keftouna laughed. This kid was definitely a special talent.

CHAPTER 6

EURO 2000

'I really thought we would win this,' Paul said, looking very disappointed and frustrated. The Pogba brothers were watching France play in another international final but this time, against Italy, they were losing 1-0 with ten minutes to go. It didn't look like the national team would win the Euro 2000 trophy to go with their 1998 World Cup triumph.

'Italy are so good in defence,' Florentin moaned. 'Fabio Cannavaro, Alessandro Nesta and Paolo Maldini are the best in the world – we just can't get past them!'

France were doing everything they could to score

an equaliser. Zidane, Thierry Henry, Sylvain Wiltord and David Trezeguet were all on the pitch but they were nearly out of time. Then in the last minute of stoppage time, Wiltord got the ball on the left side of the penalty area. The Italian defence looked tired as he took his time and fired a shot across goal. It wasn't the best strike but the ball slipped under the goalkeeper and into the goal.

'Yes!' Paul shouted, jumping up off the sofa to celebrate. 'We just need to get the golden goal now!' A new rule meant that if a team scored in extra time, the game ended straight away. It made things even more exciting.

'Come on *Les Bleus*!' Mathias shouted at the TV screen.

Just before the end of the first-half of extra time, Robert Pirès ran down the left wing and dribbled past three defenders. His cross into the box landed at Trezeguet's feet – this was the big chance that France were waiting for. Should he take a touch to control the ball? No, there were two defenders around him. He had to be quick. Trezeguet hit the ball as hard as he could and it rocketed into the top of the net.

'What a goal!' Paul shouted as the Pogba brothers danced around the living room. Everyone would be trying to score 'a Trezeguet' at Renardière for weeks.

The French players linked arms and ran to thank their fans. Paul loved the national team, and the midfield in particular. The balance was brilliant: the intelligence of Didier Deschamps, plus the strength of Patrick Vieira and the skill of Zidane. It was a winning combination. Every time he watched them play, Paul learnt new lessons about becoming a complete midfielder.

'I want to be all three of them!' he told his brothers. Henry and Trezeguet were Mathias's heroes and Florentin loved Desailly in defence. 'I'm a leader like Deschamps, I win the ball like Vieira and then I create goals like Zidane.'

Paul never even considered the possibility that he might not become a professional footballer. As long as he worked as hard as he could on tactics and technique, he knew that he would get there. He was so focused on achieving his goal that any defeat in a game was very painful. If US Roissy lost a match, Paul usually left the pitch in tears.

'Don't worry, it's just one loss,' Coach Keftouna told him, putting an arm around his shoulder. 'Even when you become the captain of France, you won't win every game. It's just not possible and so you have to learn to be a good loser.'

'I bet Zizou isn't a good loser!' Paul replied angrily. 'He wants to win every game!'

'Yes, but he still shakes hands with the other team, even after a defeat. That's good sportsmanship. And he certainly doesn't storm off the pitch!'

It was Paul's dream to be an international footballer. Because of their parents, the Pogbas would be able to play for Guinea or France. They were proud of their African heritage but France was where they had played all of their football. Plus, Guinea never got to the World Cup finals.

'If you're good enough to play for France, then you should play for France,' Yeo told her youngest son one day. Even at the age of seven, it was clear that Paul was better than his twin brothers. Everyone who watched him play said that he was a special talent. 'You could win lots of trophies with *Les Bleus*.'

Paul nodded eagerly – he wanted to win everything and follow in the footsteps of Zidane, Vieira and Deschamps.

CHAPTER 7

FOOTBALL MAD

'Djibril Cissé is definitely the best player in France,' Mamadou argued. 'He's so fast and he's always got a cool new hairstyle.'

'What about Juninho?' Habib, a Lyon fan, asked. 'His free kicks are amazing!'

'I prefer Pauleta,' said Bordeaux fan Nabil. 'He's such a good goalscorer.'

'I still love Sonny Anderson,' Ounoussou added. 'I know he's getting old but he's awesome.'

'No, you're all wrong,' Paul told his friends. 'Ronaldinho is the best!'

Although Paul still idolised Zidane, his favourite player in the French Ligue 1 was by now Paris

Saint-Germain's new Brazilian attacker, Ronaldinho.
Defenders got dizzy watching his magic feet as he
did lots of tricks and step-overs. And Ronaldinho
always played with a big smile on his face. He was a
born entertainer and Paul loved that.

Paul was totally football mad. Every morning
at school, he sat in class counting the minutes
until lunchtime. Why? Because then he could
play football. Every afternoon at school, he sat in
class counting the minutes until home-time. Why?
Because then he could play football. He ran home as
fast as he could to play in Renardière, then straight
from Renardière to training at US Roissy, and then
back to Renardière to play until it was too dark to see
the ball, and Yeo told him he had to go to bed. Only
the promise of food and the fear of his mum could
drag him away.

'Don't you ever get bored of kicking a ball around
all of the time?' Yeo asked him one day.

Paul looked confused, as if it was the stupidest
question he had ever heard. 'There's nothing boring
about football!' he told her.

And if he wasn't playing the sport, Paul was talking about it – with his teammates at US Roissy, with his classmates at school, and with his brothers at home. When their mum complained that they never talked about anything else, Paul looked surprised. 'What else is there to talk about?' he asked.

Paul was only eight years old but when his teacher asked him what he wanted to be when he was older, he said confidently, 'I'm going to be a professional footballer.' He never even thought about being a doctor, or a fireman.

Very few youngsters went on to become professional footballers but Paul was improving all the time. He always believed in himself and he was determined to get to the top. At US Roissy, he was the leader but it was a team effort. The players were all very good friends and they worked hard for each other on the pitch.

Coach Keftouna knew exactly how to get the best out of Paul. When he dribbled too much with the ball or did too many tricks, he was strict with him.

'I know you think you're Ronaldinho but you're

not,' Keftouna told him in front of all his teammates. 'Stop messing around and help us to win this match.'

If the team was losing or drawing at half-time, he spoke to his star player alone. 'We need more from you,' Keftouna said, as Paul drank some water. 'So far, you've been good but not good enough. I know how well you can play and your teammates are relying on you.'

With the responsibility of the team on his shoulders, Paul raised his game to the next level. He didn't want to let his best friends down.

'Boys, I've got some news for you,' Keftouna said at the end of a training session one day. 'We've got a big match coming up... at the Stade de France!'

Paul and his friends couldn't believe it. Only three years ago, they had all watched on TV as the French national team won the World Cup at the Stade de France. Now, they would be playing there in front of thousands of people before the French Cup Final.

'Congratulations, this is a very big opportunity for you,' Paul's dad Antoine said to him. 'There will be lots of people there looking for the next big thing.'

Some of his teammates couldn't sleep the night before but Paul was as calm as ever. He never got nervous – what was there to be nervous about? He had the chance to shine and impress the world.

'This is going to be the best day of my life!' Paul told his mum as he left the apartment to join the rest of the team for the coach trip to the stadium.

'Good luck!' Yeo said as she waved to him from the doorway. She knew her son would be a star as always.

As they got off the coach, the stadium towered above them.

'It looks like a massive spaceship!' Nabil said as they stared up at the huge concrete structure.

'How many people can fit in the stadium?' Mamadou asked with his mouth wide open in awe.

'Eighty thousand,' Coach Keftouna replied, 'but I doubt there will be that many watching you lot!'

'You never know,' Paul joked. 'We *are* pretty good!'

Coach Keftouna handed out their new football shirts for the day. They were nice red Adidas shirts but there was one problem. Paul was one of the tallest in the team and it looked way too big even on him.

'I think these are extra-large, Coach!' Ounoussou complained.

'More like extra-extra-extra-extra-extra-large!' Habib added. 'You could get three of me in here!'

Everyone was laughing but Paul was already focused on the game. What would it be like playing on such a big pitch? He would need to do even more running than usual. After a quick team photo, it was time for kick-off.

'Come on boys, we can win this!' Paul shouted as the team walked on to the pitch. He had never before stepped out on such perfect grass. It felt like a carpet and the ball rolled quickly across it. There were no odd bounces like on the pitch at Renardière.

Paul was US Roissy's best performer but their opponents were bigger and stronger than them. Some of his teammates got scared by the challenge, but Paul loved every minute of it. He fought hard in every challenge and showed off some of his skills in attack. He didn't want the game to end.

'Well played today,' Coach Keftouna said at the final whistle, putting his arm around Paul. He could see how disappointed he was to be on the losing side. 'Don't worry. If you keep on learning and improving, that definitely won't be your only appearance on a professional football pitch.'

CHAPTER 8

US TORCY

'Wow, that kid is really special,' Brahim Tlili said to the US Roissy Under-13s coach Bijou Tati after yet another victory. Paul was getting taller and better every week, and the Under-19s coach was very impressed. He had it all – strength, speed, skill and most importantly, desire. 'You can see he's so determined to be the best.'

Tati nodded. Paul had always been a very good youngster but since turning ten, there was no stopping him. He was more ambitious than ever and he had added goal-scoring to his tackling, dribbling and passing. He dominated every game, as if he was three years older than everyone else. But Tlili wasn't the only person who had noticed Paul's development. More and more youth scouts were turning up to watch their matches. They were calling him 'the new Vieira'. For how much longer could US Roissy hold on to their superstar?

'It's not every day that you see such a talented all-round midfielder,' Tati told Tlili. 'In today's game, everyone is desperately chasing that kind of player. He's a rare gem indeed!'

Paul was really happy at US Roissy. The club felt like home and he loved playing alongside his best friends every week. It was so much fun and he was really grateful for all of the coaching and support. However, he knew that it was important to challenge himself and he felt ready to play at a higher level. His dad agreed.

'It's time to get serious,' Antoine said. 'I believe that you're too good for this team.'

Yeo felt the same way but she wanted to keep her son's feet on the ground. Paul was very good but he had a long way to go and he needed to stay humble.

'Do you think you're a superstar now?' she asked

when she returned home one day to find dirty dishes everywhere and Paul sitting on the sofa with his feet up on the table. 'If this place isn't tidy in the next ten minutes, you won't be playing next week.'

Five minutes later, the apartment was back to normal. Yeo was very proud of her sons. On the Renardière estate, it was easy for kids to get involved in drugs and crime but Paul, Mathias and Florentin were well-behaved boys. They never caused trouble. They were proud Muslims and Yeo made sure that they went to the local mosque regularly.

'Be a good person first, and a great footballer second,' she often told them. The Pogba brothers knew that it was a very bad idea to upset their mum.

When Paul turned twelve years old, everyone agreed that it was finally time for him to leave US Roissy. It would be sad to see him go after seven great years but it was the best thing for Paul's career. He needed to progress to the next stage and he couldn't do that at US Roissy. Ligue 2 team Le Havre were very interested but that would mean him moving three hours away. Yeo didn't think that her son was ready for that yet.

'He's still too young,' she said. 'Everything he loves is here: his friends and his family.'

So instead, Tati contacted US Torcy, the best youth team in the area.

'I've got a kid here that you need to come and look at,' he told Stéphane Albe, their manager. 'He's incredible and he only lives twenty minutes away from your stadium. We've got a game on Saturday – come along, you won't regret it.'

Albe had heard the name 'Paul Pogba' before but people were always telling him about 'the next big thing'. Most of the time, such a player turned out to be very disappointing – a skilful player who thought he was already the best in the world, or a tall, strong boy who wasn't that good at football.

But not this time. This kid was a born athlete, gliding around the pitch with the style and intelligence of a much older player. Was he really an Under-13? The scout couldn't believe it. His vision was excellent – he knew exactly when to pass and exactly where his teammates would be. He would be a brilliant signing for US Torcy. At the end of the game, Albe spoke to Tati and then to Paul.

'Well played today! You're exactly the kind of talent that we're looking for at US Torcy,' he said. 'Our youth teams work very hard and they play at a high level. You'll learn a lot and we can make you a better player. Would you like to come down and train with us?'

'That sounds great!' Paul replied with a big smile on his face. This was the first step towards the top of world football. He couldn't wait to tell everyone the great news.

'Congratulations!' Mamadou said when he found out. Paul's US Roissy teammates were pleased for their friend but they would miss him a lot. 'Just don't forget about us when you're playing in the Champions League.'

Paul laughed. 'I promise I won't!'

CHAPTER 9

LE HAVRE

Le Havre were disappointed to see Paul sign for US Torcy but they didn't give up.

'Keep watching him,' Mohamed Chacha, their youth coach, told his scouts. 'That kid is the real deal. Soon, he'll be ready to join an even bigger club and we want to be at the front of the queue.'

Paul enjoyed life at US Torcy. It was a nice friendly club and it was still close to home. After training, he could still get back to Renardière for an hour's football on the estate with his friends and his brothers.

'Oh here comes our local superstar!' Nabil joked as Paul threw his kitbag down and joined in. 'It's such an honour to have you here!'

Paul laughed and took a bow. Mathias kicked the ball at him and then they returned to the all-important business of the match.

The standard of football at US Torcy was definitely higher than at US Roissy. The coaches pushed him hard but Paul loved the new challenge and soon he was easily their best player. He was the tallest in the team and his long legs seemed to reach every tackle first. Once he got the ball, some people expected him to be a bit clumsy but he had the quickest feet around. He had so many tricks and skills that opponents had no idea what he would do next.

'Wow, I've never seen such a complete midfielder at that age!' Coach Albe told his assistants after another match-winning performance from Paul. 'Is there anything he can't do?'

His assistants shook their heads. He was the best young player they had ever worked with. Paul had only been there for a few months but already US Torcy were worried about losing him.

'How many scouts turned up to today's game?' Albe asked with a frown on his face.

'At least ten, maybe more,' one assistant replied. 'That guy from Le Havre is still coming to every match!'

Paul tried to ignore all of the gossip and rumours and focus on his football. The US Torcy coaches were teaching him more and more about controlling the game from midfield. But Le Havre were a very good team with a great reputation for developing young players. If they tried to sign him again, he would have a difficult decision to make.

'How did Paul play at the weekend?' Chacha asked his scout at their Monday morning meeting.

'He was brilliant,' the scout replied. He looked very excited. 'He was everywhere, running from box to box all game long. He set up two goals and he nearly scored from about thirty yards! Even in the last few weeks, he's improved.'

Chacha nodded. 'Okay, I'll come and watch his next match.'

If he didn't know better, he would have thought that Paul was playing with much younger kids. And it wasn't just because of his height. While the other players chased the ball around the pitch and kicked it anywhere, Paul was very calm. The whole game slowed down when he was in possession and Chacha could tell that he was really thinking about what to do next. Wearing the captain's armband, he was playing like a leader.

'Very impressive,' Chacha said to himself. As he watched, he made notes in his notebook:

'*Skinny but lots of power in his legs*'

'*Very mature for his age*'

'*Takes risks with the ball, but good risks*'

As the football season came to an end, Chacha decided to make his move.

'Paul is a very talented young player and we believe that it's the right time for him to move to a bigger club like Le Havre,' he told Paul's dad Antoine at a meeting. 'We look after our kids very well – just ask Vikash Dhorasoo and Jean-Alain Boumsong!'

Dhorasoo and Boumsong were both top French internationals who had started their careers at Le Havre. Antoine knew that it would be a very smart move for his son. Paul had already outgrown US Torcy but joining a big Ligue 1 club like Marseille or Paris Saint-Germain might be a mistake. He needed close care and attention, and Le Havre would be perfect.

'Let me speak to Paul and we'll be in touch soon,' Antoine said.

'Mum, it would be very cool to play for Le Havre but what about my friends?' Paul asked at dinner one night. 'It's really far away and so I would never get to play with them on the estate!'

'You would still see them, I promise,' Yeo reassured her youngest son. 'Mathias and Florentin are moving to Spain – at least you will still be in France! It's only a few hours.'

Paul thought long and hard about the offer. In the end, it all came down to his ambition. He wanted to become one of the best players in the world, and to achieve that, he would need to keep challenging himself. Le Havre were a professional club playing in the second highest league in France. That was a big deal.

'Dad, I've made my decision,' Paul told Antoine at the weekend. 'I want to sign for Le Havre.'

US Torcy were very sad to lose Paul but they couldn't compete. Chacha was delighted with his new signing. The fourteen-year-old boy had so much potential and he was so determined to succeed.

'I think I play a bit like Vieira, a bit like Zidane and a bit like Ronaldinho,' Paul told him on the way to his new club's stadium, the Stade Océane.

Chacha looked to see if the youngster was joking but Paul was deadly serious. When it came to football, there was no joking.

'Wow, I love that confidence!' the youth coach said with a huge smile on his face.

CHAPTER 10

CAPTAIN OF FRANCE

'Hello stranger!' Mamadou shouted, giving Paul a massive hug. Their special handshake lasted almost a whole minute but they both remembered every single part. They looked like long-lost friends as they laughed and talked next to the pitch where they had grown up together. 'I haven't seen you in weeks – I was beginning to think that you thought you were too good for us now!'

'I'm sorry,' Paul replied. He really missed his mates but his life was very, very busy. 'I'm travelling and playing football so much at the moment. It's great but there's not a lot of time to come home and chill out with you guys.'

'You're forgiven!' Mamadou smiled.

'How are things at US Roissy?' Paul asked. His first club would always have a special place in his heart.

'Don't worry, we're surviving without you. But more importantly, how is everything at Le Havre?'

'It's really good, thanks,' Paul replied. 'At first, I was pretty nervous – some of the kids there are amazing! But you know me; I'm not scared of anything. I'm improving all the time.'

'That's awesome! And my mum told me that you're playing for France too?'

Paul looked a little embarrassed. Yeo had always taught him to be modest about his achievements. 'Yes, but how did she hear about that?'

Mamadou laughed and rolled his eyes. 'How do you think? Your mum is very proud of you – and so are we!'

'Thanks mate, things are happening so quickly,' Paul said, taking a long, deep breath. Sometimes, it all still felt like a dream.

When Paul first arrived at the Le Havre training facility, he couldn't believe it. They had all of the most modern fitness equipment and the changing rooms looked like a hotel. It was a very long way from US Roissy.

'We have big plans here at Le Havre,' Chacha explained to Paul on that first tour. 'Our brilliant youth team feeds our senior team. They finished sixth last season but our aim is to get promoted this time. We're ready for Ligue 1!'

That was the kind of ambition that Paul loved and thanks to star striker Guillaume Hoarau, Le Havre did indeed run away with the Ligue 2 title.

'He scored twenty-eight goals – that's almost twice as many as Cissé!' Paul said to his teammates. Hoarau was their hero and they often stayed behind to watch him practise. They wanted to learn as much as possible from him.

'Keep improving and any one of you could be the next Guillaume Hoarau,' Chacha told his youth team. It was great motivation for them all but Paul was particularly excited. He loved being in an environment where the line-up wasn't just decided by age and experience; first and foremost, it was about talent.

Paul settled in very quickly at Le Havre and in his second season, Chacha made him captain.

'You're a natural leader – you fight hard for the team and the others follow your example,' the coach said, offering him the armband.

Paul was delighted and he couldn't wait to tell his dad the good news.

'That's great, son,' Antoine said proudly. 'You have a lot of responsibility now.'

Paul didn't mind the pressure; in fact, it seemed to make him play even better. In the Under-16 league, Le Havre were up against big, heavyweight clubs, including Lyon, Lens and Nancy. The team would have to be at their very best to compete.

'If we work together, we can do this!' Paul told his teammates before the season kicked off. They all listened carefully to their new captain. 'We're the underdogs but it's our time to shine.'

In the centre of midfield, Paul was at the heart of the team, controlling everything. He battled bravely to win the ball and then moved his team forward up the pitch. When he got the chance, he still showed off some tricks but only when it wasn't too dangerous. He encouraged the others and gave them instructions too. Under his leadership, Le Havre surprised everyone except their coach.

'This is the best team I've ever worked with,' Chacha told them. They were second in the league, with only Lens ahead of them. 'It's all about belief – we have to believe!'

Paul certainly believed – in his coach, in his teammates and especially in himself. He was on the path to greatness; he was sure of it. He just needed to keep doing what he was doing. Not only was he playing for the France Under-16s but he was also their captain now.

'If you stay disciplined, you can be one of the best in the world,' Guy Ferrier, the coach, told him at their training camp. 'When you shine, everyone around you shines. You have everything you need to succeed. I'm showing a lot of faith in you – prove me right.'

'Thanks, boss,' Paul replied with a big smile on his face. 'It's a real honour to lead my country. I won't let you down.'

Three years earlier, he had been playing for his small, local club and now he was the captain of France for his age group. The best clubs in France were interested in him and so were Manchester United, Chelsea and Arsenal in England. It seemed crazy but it was really happening. Yes, as he told Mamadou, things were moving very quickly. Paul had no idea what might happen next.

CHAPTER 11

MOVING TO MANCHESTER

Manchester United had scouts all over the world, watching lots and lots of football matches in the hope of discovering a new superstar. As one of the biggest clubs in the world, they wanted to find the biggest new talents, and sign them before anyone else could beat them to it. That's how they signed Cristiano Ronaldo and that's how they signed Paul too.

David Friio had been a footballer for Plymouth Argyle in England but when he retired, he moved back home to France and started scouting. There were lots of great players in Ligue 1 and Ligue 2 and they were usually cheaper than players in Italy or

Spain. David had only been in the job for a few years
but he already had a good eye for a bargain.

'Give me ten minutes and I'll tell you if a kid is
special,' he liked to tell people.

David travelled all over the country in his search
but Le Havre was right at the top of his list. The
club had a brilliant reputation for developing young
players, and in 2009, they had one of France's most
highly-rated players: the Under-16 national team
captain, Paul Pogba.

'Right, let's see how good he really is,' David
said to himself as he took his seat in the stands of
the Stade Océane. There was a big crowd and he
recognised scouts from other big clubs; word about
Paul was clearly spreading very quickly.

The first thing David noticed about Paul was his
height. As he came out on to the pitch, the boy
looked about a foot taller than all of his teammates.
His legs looked long enough to stretch all the way
across the pitch to win the ball. He was still very
skinny but building up strength was the easy part.
Maybe this really was 'the new Patrick Vieira'.

As soon as the game kicked off, Paul was at the centre of everything. For a lanky teenager, he looked so classy on the ball. His passing was calm and clever, and it was hard to tell if he was right or left-footed. Sometimes he got caught too far up the pitch but they could still work on his positioning. Manchester United would be the perfect place for him to learn.

Just before half-time, the ball came to Paul about thirty yards from goal. The defenders expected him to pass the ball into the box but instead he took one touch and fired a powerful shot into the top corner. *Boooooooooooooom!* The goalkeeper barely saw the ball as it whizzed past him.

'Wow,' David mumbled to himself. He had an urgent phone call to make.

'I've found an incredible talent and we need to act fast,' he told United's youth coach, Paul McGuinness.

'Okay, what position does he play?' Paul asked. It was a long time since he had heard one of their scouts sound so excited about a young player.

'He plays in central midfield but he's got

everything. He runs, he tackles, he passes, he dribbles and he's got a bullet of a shot too!'

'A new Scholesy?' Paul asked. For years, Manchester United had been looking for someone to eventually replace club legend, Paul Scholes. They were very difficult shoes to fill. A midfielder who could defend, create chances and score goals was very, very difficult to find. In fact, it was almost impossible.

'Maybe not but trust me, he's the best kid that I've ever seen in that position at that age,' David replied. He was desperate for the club to take a chance on Paul. 'There are Arsenal and Chelsea scouts here tonight, and probably quite a few others too.'

'Okay, let me speak to Fergie,' Paul said. Sir Alex Ferguson, the United manager, always made the final decision. 'We might be visiting you in France very soon.'

It didn't take long to convince everyone at the club that young Paul was Manchester United material. The harder thing was convincing him and his family that Manchester United was the best place for him to make progress. Juventus, Lyon, Chelsea and Arsenal were also battling for Paul's signature. He was the hottest new talent in Europe and he had a lot of offers to choose from.

'Your son has excellent potential,' Ferguson told Yeo at their apartment. A home visit was a sure sign that Fergie was very serious about a player. 'With our facilities and our coaches, we can turn Paul into one of the best midfielders in the world.'

Manchester United's youth academy was world-famous for producing great players like David Beckham, Ryan Giggs and Paul Scholes, and Ferguson himself had come all the way to speak to Yeo and Antoine. Paul would be in very safe hands, and they were very impressed by Ferguson's offer.

'What do you think?' they asked their son. They would do whatever made him happy. Living in England would be a big change for a sixteen-year-old from Renardière.

Paul took his time to make up his mind. This was a massive step in his career and he wanted to make the right choice. Eventually, he was ready to reveal his answer.

'I want to go to Manchester United!' He told his parents with a big smile on his face. He still couldn't believe this was really happening. He had always believed in himself but now one of the biggest teams in the world, the eleven-time Premier League Champions, believed in him too.

Le Havre were very disappointed to see Paul leave but there was nothing that they could do, except wish their star youngster the best.

'Good luck and never forget where you've come from,' the club president, Jean-Pierre Louvel, told him as they said goodbye. 'Work hard and make the most of your talent.'

Paul nodded and thanked Louvel for all of his support and guidance over the previous few years. There was no way that he was going to waste this opportunity. His parents and coaches had always inspired him to never stop learning new things. He couldn't wait to move to Manchester but he had one big concern.

'Mum, I'm worried about getting homesick,' he told Yeo as they prepared for his big move. 'What if I don't like England? I hear the weather is rubbish!'

Yeo laughed. 'Don't worry – I'm coming to Manchester with you!'

CHAPTER 12

TOP DOG

'Does anyone know anything about this French
kid we've just signed?' Ravel Morrison asked his
Manchester United Under-18 teammates at the club's
Carrington training centre. Ravel was the star of the
youth team and he wanted to know everything about
his new competition.

'I hear he's already got his own physio and
dietician,' Jesse Lingard replied. 'He's only sixteen
but he's basically already a professional!'

'I played against him for the Republic of Ireland
Under-17s last year,' defender Sean McGinty added.
'He's brilliant!'

'We'll see about that,' Ravel said grumpily. He was

pleased that the youth team was getting better but he was the top dog and he would make sure that the squad's young newcomer knew this.

'Everybody, this is our new player, Paul Pogba,' coach Paul McGuinness told the squad. 'He's come from Le Havre in France, so please make him feel welcome.'

'He's a giant!' Jesse whispered to Ravel. 'Are you sure he's only sixteen?'

Before the training session started, Paul was all smiles and laughter. His English wasn't very good yet but he wanted to show his new teammates that he was a fun guy to have around. They would be spending a lot of time together and he knew how important a good group spirit was. If they were friends off the pitch, they would play better on the pitch.

But as soon as the practice drills began, Paul was totally focused. His smile disappeared and there was a fire in his eyes. He never stopped moving and pushed himself to the limit. Paul was desperate to impress everyone.

McGuinness watched his new player carefully. He

was surprised by the elegance of the lanky teenager. Despite those long legs, Paul had brilliant footwork and lots of skills. And he had plenty of confidence too. It was only his first day at Manchester United but he was already challenging Ravel's status as top dog. The big game at the end of training was going to be very interesting.

When it came to proper matches, McGuinness was strict with his players but in the training games, he encouraged them to try new skills and have fun. He believed it was an important part of a youngster's development, and the lads loved it. McGuinness made sure that Paul and Ravel were on opposite teams.

Paul got the ball and nutmegged one player, then flicked the ball over the next player's head. He controlled the ball perfectly, dropped his shoulder to confuse the defender and then played a no-look pass to Jesse, who scored.

'Wow, Paul's got unbelievable tekkers!' Michael Keane shouted.

Ravel accepted the challenge. He got the ball and ran forward. He did a few stepovers and then a

Maradona turn through a defender's legs. It was on his weaker right foot but he scored with a *rabona*, putting his left foot behind his right to shoot.

'That's a worldie!' Michael's twin brother Will shouted back.

The match became Paul vs Ravel and it was really entertaining. Elasticos, Cruyff turns, rainbow flicks, drag-backs – they did them all. McGuinness couldn't stop smiling. In Paul, he had found a player that would really get the best out of Ravel.

At the end of the game, Paul was exhausted but he had really enjoyed himself. He could tell that he was going to have a good time at Manchester United.

'Well played, that was unbelievable!' he said to Ravel, shaking his hand.

'Yeah, you're amazing!' Ravel replied. 'We'll be unstoppable this season.'

Off the pitch, Ravel and Paul became really good friends and Jesse was the third musketeer. They all loved rap music and dancing, and Paul felt like he was back at Renardière with Mamadou, Habib, Nabil and Ounoussou.

'Have you heard this new song?' Paul asked, sharing his headphones as they sat together at the back of the team bus. Soon, the three of them were singing along and having a dance competition.

On the pitch, Ravel and Paul were teammates but also rivals. If Ravel did a great trick, Paul would try to do an even better one; if Paul scored a good goal, Ravel would try to score two good goals. Both players took lots of exciting risks with the ball but if a skill went wrong, they always worked hard to make up for their mistake. Thanks to Paul and Ravel's healthy competition, Manchester United finished top of their group in the Premier Academy League.

In the semi-finals they faced Arsenal. The score was 1-1 after extra-time but Manchester United lost on penalties.

'Don't worry, we'll win it next year,' Paul told his teammates in the changing room after the match. Everyone was really disappointed but they would get another opportunity. They were still young and learning. 'We just need to take our chances next time.'

McGuinness was very impressed by Paul's attitude. He liked to joke around and show off sometimes but he was a born winner. As soon as the game kicked off, Paul gave 110 per cent for the team. McGuinness knew that it wouldn't be long before he was playing for the first team. Ravel had already made his debut and Paul was never far behind him. After a few months of the 2010–11 season, Paul received some good news.

'Congratulations, you've been called up to the reserve team,' McGuinness told him after training. 'You'll be playing with the big boys now!'

Paul was really pleased – it was a big step-up for a seventeen-year-old. Playing against much older players would be a real challenge, especially in the centre of midfield where there was lots of tough tackling. Paul was building up more and more muscle but he was still quite skinny. Luckily, nothing scared him.

'So what if they're stronger than me?!' he told his mum before his first match against Bolton Wanderers. 'The important question is: are they better than me? I doubt it!'

Paul still played for the academy team in its most important competition, the FA Youth Cup. Against Portsmouth in the third round, the ball came to him twenty-five yards from goal. Paul knew he was a brilliant long-range shooter and so without even taking a touch to control it, he fired the ball towards goal. *Booooooooooom!* The goalkeeper had no chance as it sailed into the top corner.

Gooooooooooooooooooooooooaaaaaaaaaaaaaaaaaaaaa llllllllllllllllllllllllllllllll!!!!!!!!!!!

As his teammates jumped on him, Paul stayed cool and put his arms up in the air. As soon as he kicked it, he knew that it was going to be a great goal.

Manchester United beat West Ham, Newcastle and Liverpool to reach the FA Youth Cup semi-final against Chelsea. In the first leg at Stamford Bridge, Manchester United were 2-0 down at half-time.

'Come on, we're so much better than this!' Paul shouted in the dressing room. 'We can't make any more sloppy mistakes. In the second half, we need to play like we normally do.'

Paul got the ball, beat one player and then did a

Maradona turn past the next. He was a long way from goal but he had space and a rocket of a shot. The ball flew through the air but the goalkeeper made a good save. 'Come on!' Paul shouted, encouraging his teammates.

A few minutes later, a corner came to the back post and Jesse shot into the net. Briefly, Manchester United were back in the game but then Chelsea scored a third. It looked like the game was over but Paul never gave up. He had one shot saved but minutes later, Jesse delivered a great cross into the box. Paul jumped highest and headed it low into the bottom corner.

'What a goal!' Jesse shouted as they celebrated. 'Now we just have to win the second leg at Old Trafford by one.'

In the end, Manchester United won the second leg 4-0 but Paul's goal had been key to keeping their hopes alive. When the pressure was on, he had been their leader.

In the final, they played Sheffield United. The away leg finished 2-2, which meant Manchester

United just needed to win at home. The team was feeling very confident.

'We've done so well to get this far,' Ravel said before kick-off. 'We just need one more great performance and the trophy is ours!'

Ravel scored two as Manchester United won 4-1. The three musketeers celebrated afterwards with the Youth Cup in their hands.

'This is the first of many for us!' Ravel said, doing a silly dance.

Paul joined in. 'Yes, but the next one will be with the senior team – we're the future of this club!'

CHAPTER 13

LEARNING FROM LEGENDS

'Boss, I know you don't want to rush things with Paul but I think he's ready,' Ole Gunnar Solskjaer told Sir Alex Ferguson. Solskjaer became a Manchester United legend when he scored in their famous 1999 Champions League final win and he was now the manager of the reserve team.

Paul's talent was the talk of the club and Ferguson knew that he shouldn't wait too long to give him a chance in the first team. Over the years, he had put his faith in so many great youngsters. Ravel, for example, had made his debut the year before. Was Paul the next big star? The only way to find out was to let him play.

'I know, we can't hold him back any longer,' Ferguson said. 'If we do, he'll leave and we really don't want that. He's exactly what we're looking for in midfield – he's tall, he's athletic and he's skilful.'

Paul had started training with the first team during the 2010–11 season. Practising with legends like Ryan Giggs and Wayne Rooney was a dream come true. Just watching them up close was an amazing experience.

'What's it like?' Adnan Januzaj asked. He was two years younger and a brilliant winger in the academy.

'The level is incredible!' Paul replied. 'It's a massive challenge but you know me – I love that!'

As a central midfielder, there was one particular player that Paul was desperate to learn from – Paul Scholes. He was thirty-six years old now but he hadn't lost any of his ability. Every single pass and shot was absolutely perfect.

'How does he do that?' Paul said to Jesse. 'He's like a robot!'

Scholesy had an amazing football brain and he was always thinking one step ahead. When he got the ball, he already knew exactly where it would go next. That was something that the teenage Paul really wanted to work on. Because he was really tall, he could shield the ball well and take his time to pick a pass. But Scholesy was quite small and so he had to make really fast decisions. There was so much still to learn if Paul wanted to be the best around.

The other thing that Paul admired about Scholesy was his desire to win.

'That guy is at the end of his career and he has won everything – eleven Premier League titles and two Champions League trophies,' he told Ravel. 'But he's still there at the end of training every day, practising. It's unbelievable!'

Paul worked harder than ever and the senior players were very impressed.

'Keep going and you'll make your debut very soon,' Patrice Evra told him. He was a top French international and he took Paul under his wing. He gave him lots of advice and sometimes had dinner with Paul and his mum. 'We really need a top-quality midfielder like you!'

When Scholesy retired at the end of the season,

there was a Paul-sized gap in the Manchester United
midfield. He enjoyed every day with the first team
but he was impatient to play an actual match for
them. He was sure that he had the ambition and
talent to fill Scholesy's big boots.

'I'm learning so much in training but I need to put
it into practice on the pitch at Old Trafford!' he told
his mum. He wanted to play in front of the amazing
crowd at the Theatre of Dreams.

'Don't worry, it will happen soon, I'm sure,' Yeo
told him. She had full confidence in her son.

Paul was given the Manchester United Number 42
shirt and ahead of the start of the League Cup, he got
the news that he was waiting for.

'Pogba will play against Leeds United,' Ferguson
told the media at a press conference.

Paul was so excited about his big day that when
he was named amongst the substitutes, he was
disappointed.

'What if I only play for ten minutes?' he
complained to Jesse. 'I need more time than that to
impress the boss!'

It was really hard watching the first half from the bench. Paul wanted to be out there playing. At half-time, Manchester United were winning 3-0. Surely the match was safe now?

'Paul, get ready,' Ferguson told him. 'You're coming on for Giggsy.'

A big smile spread across Paul's face – he would have a full forty-five minutes to show what he could do. He couldn't wait and he wasn't nervous at all.

'It's my time to shine,' he thought to himself as he took his tracksuit off and pulled his socks up.

In the second half, Paul didn't stop running. Alongside Michael Carrick in midfield, he felt very comfortable. At first, Paul tried to keep things simple. When he got the ball, he looked up and played the pass straight away before moving into space again. But as he grew more confident, he dribbled forward and tried to get into the penalty area. When the final whistle sounded, he was exhausted but he wasn't ready to leave the field. He could have played another ninety minutes.

'Well played,' Ferguson told him, giving him a pat on the back.

Paul was pretty pleased with his performance but he knew he could do much more. He just needed regular game time. In the fourth round against Aldershot, Manchester United were 3-0 up again and Paul came on after sixty minutes. There was nothing to lose and everything to gain. Ten minutes later, he took a shot from just outside the penalty area. *Booooooooooom!* This time, the ball flew way over the crossbar – but Paul was just getting started.

'Next time!' he said to himself as he ran back to get ready for the goal kick.

Step by step, Paul was getting closer to the big time. He was doing well and impressing Ferguson with his calmness and maturity in midfield. The League Cup was a good learning curve but he was already thinking ahead to his next target.

'I'm ready to make my Premier League debut now,' he told Jesse at training. And he was definitely not the only person at Old Trafford who believed that.

CHAPTER 14

FIRST-TEAM FRUSTRATIONS

'Scholesy's back!'

The rumour was spreading throughout the club.
Paul Scholes had only retired six months earlier but
the Manchester United legend was returning because
of an injury crisis. With Rio Ferdinand and Nemanja
Vidić out, Michael Carrick was playing in defence. So
who would replace Michael in midfield?

Paul had very mixed feelings about Scholesy's
arrival. On the one hand, it was great to see his
hero back in training but on the other hand, why
didn't Ferguson trust him? Paul was ready to
become Scholes's replacement but the manager
preferred to bring a thirty-seven-year-old back into

the team rather than give a very promising eighteen-year-old an opportunity. It was disappointing and frustrating.

On New Year's Eve 2011, Manchester United were at home to Blackburn Rovers and Scholesy wasn't yet fit to play. Tom Cleverley and Darron Gibson were also unavailable.

'Congratulations on making the matchday squad,' Jesse told Paul excitedly. 'You're about to get your chance!'

He really hoped that his friend was right. Paul had been waiting for months to play in the Premier League and he was starting to lose hope. After starring in the Youth Cup victory, he thought great things were about to happen. Ferguson had told him several times that he was nearly there but he couldn't be a top prospect forever. He needed to play regular first-team football.

He was full of hope and excitement as the starting line-up was announced:

De Gea, Valencia, Carrick, Jones, Evra, Nani, Rafael, Park, Welbeck, Hernandez, Berbatov...

Paul's heart sank. He wasn't in the eleven. Instead, he would have to sit on the bench again.

'I can't believe it!' he told his agent, Mino Raiola, on the phone before the match. He was furious. 'Rafael is a right-back and Ji-Sung Park is a winger – why are they playing in central midfield instead of me?'

'I have no idea but stay calm,' Mino replied. 'I'm sure you'll come on in the second half.'

But when Javier Hernández came off at half-time, it was Anderson that came on in midfield, not Paul. The match finished 3-2 to Blackburn and Paul didn't play a single minute. It was definitely his worst day at Manchester United.

He took a few days to think about things but he still wasn't happy. 'If they won't give me a game when there aren't any other central midfielders available, there's no point me being here!' Paul told his agent.

Mino knew that youngsters were often too impatient but he couldn't understand why Manchester United were treating Paul like this. He wasn't a difficult character; his attitude was always excellent. He was one of the best young players in the world and he just wanted to play football. What was the problem?

Manchester United wanted Paul to sign a new contract but he wasn't sure that he wanted to stay.

'I love my teammates and the club feels like home but I'm tired of being a player with "potential",' Paul continued. 'I'm not a star for the future; I'm a star for the present!'

'I agree and so do many other clubs,' Mino told him. 'Juventus are ready to make you a great offer and they say you'll be a regular starter.'

It was very tempting, particularly as Paul's biggest hero, Zinedine Zidane, had played for the Italian club. 'Let's see what happens in the next few months,' he said to his agent.

At the end of January 2012, Paul finally made his Premier League debut. Against Stoke, he ran on to the pitch to replace Javier. The noise of the 75,000 fans at Old Trafford was incredible. It was the best feeling of Paul's life so far.

'It's my time to shine!' he said to himself.

'Get forward as much as you can,' Scholesy told him.

Paul nodded happily. He was determined to make a name for himself. For the last twenty minutes, he was involved in everything. He took set pieces, he won free kicks and he had a couple of shots too. The Manchester United fans cheered loudly – they loved to see exciting young players in their team.

'That was amazing,' Paul said to goalkeeper Ben Amos at the final whistle. 'I want to do that every day for the rest of my life!'

'Me too!' Ben replied. 'A clean sheet on my debut – that's a pretty good start.'

After the game, Ferguson had lots of praise for Paul. 'He did really well. It's hard to believe that he's only eighteen years old,' he told the media.

But Paul didn't play at all against Chelsea, Liverpool, Norwich or Tottenham. Finally, six weeks later, he came on for the last twenty minutes against West Brom. He did his best to make an impact but Manchester United were already winning 2-0. The same thing happened a week later against Wolves: he was not on the pitch at kick-off.

'These games are already over!' Paul moaned. 'Why can't I just start a game?'

Everyone at Manchester United knew that he was unhappy and they were worried that their best young talent was about to leave. Patrice came to speak to him and his family.

'If Paul stays here, he will become a legend. He just needs to be patient.'

'But I'm not sixteen anymore!' Paul replied. 'Lionel Messi had played more than twenty-five league games by the time he turned nineteen. I've only played three! Cristiano Ronaldo played lots of games for Manchester United when he was eighteen. If I want to keep improving, I need to play every week.'

Paul had already made up his mind and in July, he signed for Juventus on a four-year contract. The Italian champions had great players like Gianluigi Buffon and Andrea Pirlo but they needed a young playmaker with lots of energy. At Manchester

United, Paul had worn the Number 42 shirt, but Juventus gave him the Number 6 shirt.

'They believe in me and that's all I want,' he told Jesse and Ravel as he said goodbye.

They were very sad to see their best friend go but they understood his decision. 'Go and become a superstar in Italy. Then come back to Manchester!'

CHAPTER 15

POGBOOM

'Wow, I've never been so tired in my life!' Paul said to teammate and fellow Frenchman Nicolas Anelka as he left the pitch after his first training session at Juventus.

Paul felt sick but he was pleased with his effort. The sessions in Italy were much longer than in England, with hours of running and strength exercises. He was still pretty thin and the club wanted him to add muscle quickly.

'The football is very physically challenging here,' Pavel Nedved told him. The Juventus legend was now the club's vice chairman, and he gave Paul lots of advice in his first few months. 'I know you have

96

the talent, but you'll need to be tough too!'

At Manchester United, Paul had spent hours watching Paul Scholes in action. At Juventus, he had a new hero to learn from: Andrea Pirlo. Like Scholesy, Andrea was nearing the end of his career but he was still amazing.

In training, Andrea calmly passed the ball across the midfield, waiting for the right moment. Suddenly, he curled a killer pass over the defence for striker Sebastian Giovinco.

'I didn't even see Sebastian's run!' Paul said to Claudio Marchisio.

'I know, I'd pay a lot of money for his eyes,' Claudio replied, laughing. 'He's got X-ray vision!'

Like Scholesy, Andrea wasn't afraid to make a mistake. If he played one bad pass, everyone knew that he would make nine excellent ones after that. Paul had that same confidence; he just needed to learn to read the game like Andrea.

'My new teammates are incredible!' he told his mum. 'I'm improving every day.'

With Andrea playing as a deep playmaker, the

other Juventus midfielders had to work really hard, running box to box to tackle and score. Paul was in his element.

'I was born to play this role!' he told Claudio after a preseason match against Benfica. He couldn't wait for the season to begin properly.

In his Serie A debut, Paul played the full ninety minutes. The atmosphere was incredible in the Juventus Stadium and they dominated from the kick-off. When Fabio Quagliarella finally scored the opening goal, Paul was the first player to join in the celebrations. He was already a key member of the squad.

Paul was protecting the defence well and playing good forward passes but he wanted to do more in attack.

'The fans haven't really seen me shoot yet!' he told Claudio.

'Yes, when are they going to see the kind of great goals we've seen you score in training?' Claudio asked.

'Very soon!' was Paul's instant reply.

Against title rivals Napoli, Juventus were 1-0 up with ten minutes to go. A second goal would really help to secure the victory. Sebaştian ran forward and his shot deflected up into the air off a defender. Paul was twenty-five yards from goal and the ball fell perfectly for him to volley. He watched it closely fall on to his left foot and then drilled his shot low into the bottom corner. *Booooooooooooom!*

Goooooooooooooooooooooaaaaaaaaaaaaaaaaaaaaaa aalllllllllllllllllllllllllllllll!!!!!!!!!!

Paul didn't go crazy; he was too cool for that. Instead, he nodded his head and pointed to the bench as if to say, 'That's what I can do!'

He was feeling more and more confident at Juventus, especially going forward into attack. Andrea, Claudio and Arturo Vidal were the first-choice midfielders but manager Antonio Conte had a lot of faith in Paul.

'You won't play every game but if you keep improving like this, it will be very difficult to leave you on the bench!'

Against Bologna, Paul curled a great shot towards

the top corner but it struck the post. A few minutes later, he directed a header just wide. He didn't give up, though. Instead, he set up the first Juventus goal with a beautiful chip pass over the defence.

'What a through-ball!' Andrea shouted as they celebrated. It was a massive compliment and it showed just how well Paul was doing.

Bologna equalised but in injury time, Paul scored a header at the back post to win the match. It was his best performance ever and the Italian newspapers went wild. *La Repubblica* called him a 'hurricane' and *La Gazzetta dello Sport* predicted that he could be even better than Patrick Vieira. Paul was delighted with the praise but he knew he had a long way to go before he could be compared to Vieira.

'Manchester United must be kicking themselves!' Florentin joked on the phone after the game. He was very proud of his younger brother's progress.

In early 2013, Juventus faced Udinese. As the first half was coming to an end, the ball came to Paul at least forty yards from goal. The easy option would be

to cross the ball into the box but Paul loved taking
risks, and he loved shooting. He took one touch and
struck the ball with the outside of his right foot. He
made it look so easy but the power was phenomenal.
Booooooooom! Before anyone knew what was
going on, the ball hit the top corner of the net.

*Goooooooooooooooooooooooaaaaaaaaaaaaaaaa
aaaaaaaaaalllllllllllllllll!!!!!!!!*

Paul's celebration was as cool as ever. He raised
his arms into the air as the crowd called out his new
nickname.

Pogboom! Pogboom! Pogboom!

In the second half, he did it again. This time, he
used his skill to get away from two defenders and
hit a thunderous strike into the bottom corner. As
the ball flew past the goalkeeper, Paul danced like he
used to back in Renardière.

The fans loved it. With his great goals, his cool
character and his dyed-blonde Mohawk and go-faster
stripes, Paul was the most exciting new player in
Europe. He loved proving people wrong. He had
never doubted his own ability but some critics had

said that he had only moved to Juventus for the money. That wasn't true; he had moved to Juventus to win, win, win and become a superstar.

CHAPTER 16

FUTURE OF FRANCE

'Our young midfielder Paul Pogba is making a great start to his career at Juventus,' the French newspapers reported in early 2013. 'The big question is: when will he win his first international cap?'

Paul had starred for France at every youth level – Under-16s, Under-17s, Under-18s and Under-19s. At the 2012 European Under-19 Championships in Estonia, the coach Pierre Mankowski had even made Paul his captain.

'We need a leader out there on the pitch,' Mankowski told him. 'I know that you have the focus and ambition to help us win this tournament.'

It was a real honour for Paul to wear the armband,

just as he had for the Under-16s a few years earlier. France had a strong squad, with Samuel Umtiti in central defence and Geoffrey Kondogbia alongside Paul in midfield. They were an athletic and powerful team, and they progressed to the semi-finals.

"Spain have got some really good attackers,' Samuel admitted as they prepared for the match. 'Jesé, Gerard Deulofeu and Paco Alcácer are all in great form.'

Paul wanted his teammates to be really positive and share his confidence. 'Yes, but we've got great defenders *and* attackers. If we play our best football, we can beat anyone.'

France took the lead halfway through the first half. From a corner, Paul rose highest but his header was blocked. Luckily, Samuel reacted first and smashed the ball into the net.

'Stay focused!' Paul shouted as the game resumed. He didn't want to see any sloppy mistakes.

After ninety minutes, the two teams were tied at 2-2. In extra time, Spain took the lead and it looked like France were heading out of the tournament. But

Paul hadn't given up. These big matches were his favourite time to shine.

As the ball moved down the left wing, Paul made a great run from the right wing all the way to the back post. The cross into the box was deflected by a defender and it seemed to be going out for a corner. But Paul stretched out his long right leg.

Gooooooooooooooooooooooooooaaaaaaaaaaaaaaaa aaalllllllllllllllllllllllll!!!!!!!!!!

Thanks to their captain, France were still in the game. It went to penalties and Paul was the first to volunteer and the first to take his penalty. He stepped up confidently and scored.

'Come on!' he shouted as he ran back to stand with his teammates on the halfway line.

Unfortunately, Samuel and Geoffrey both missed their penalties and it was Spain who went through to the final. It was a heartbreaking end for France and Paul hated losing but he was very proud of his team.

'Keep your heads up boys, we showed incredible spirit,' he told them in the dressing room afterwards.

Paul loved playing for his country and so he was

very happy to hear people saying that he should be called up to the senior team.

'I'm waiting by the phone!' he joked with his brothers. Florentin and Mathias had decided to play for Guinea but Paul was holding out for France.

He didn't have to wait long. Coach Didier Deschamps, one of Paul's heroes from the 1998 World Cup-winning team, named him in the squad to face Georgia and Spain.

'This is the best news ever!' Paul told his dad. 'I'll be training with Franck Ribéry, Karim Benzema and Patrice too.'

Ever since he was a young boy back in Renardière watching the 1998 World Cup victory, Paul had always dreamed of becoming a French international player. It was the greatest honour in football to represent your country at the highest level. For the first time ever, Paul felt a little nervous as he arrived at the training camp – but not for long.

'Hello stranger!' Patrice joked, giving him a big hug. It was nice to meet up with his old Manchester United teammate again.

'Hello, are you surviving without me?' Paul asked.

'We're top of the league!' Patrice replied with a big smile.

Paul was happy just to be in the squad; when he found out that he would be in the starting eleven for the Georgia match, he was delighted. Great things kept happening so fast.

Walking out on the Stade de France pitch in his France tracksuit was one of the best moments of Paul's life. He played the whole ninety minutes and they won 3-1. Some youngsters might have been scared about making their international debut but not Paul.

'Playing in the big matches is the best feeling in the world,' he told his mum. 'Mamso, this is why I became a professional footballer!'

Yeo loved to hear her son sounding so excited. After a tough time in Manchester, he was really flourishing in Italy. When a coach believed in him, he played with more energy and enthusiasm.

Paul thought that he would be on the bench for the second, bigger match against Spain but to his surprise he was in the starting line-up again. Against the World Champions, Paul played a disciplined role, protecting his defence. But after sixty goalless minutes, Spain scored.

'We were looking so solid!' Paul thought to himself as he kicked the grass in frustration. He was really disappointed.

Paul had always had a hot temper but most of the time he could control it. Unfortunately, as France missed several chances to equalise, Paul grew angrier and angrier. He was very competitive and he really didn't want to lose to Spain again.

With fifteen minutes to go, Paul got a yellow card for a heavy challenge on Xabi Alonso. It should have been a warning but two minutes later, he slid in for a late tackle on Xavi. The referee showed him another yellow card and then the red. Paul walked slowly off the pitch and down the tunnel.

Once he had calmed down, he was very ashamed of himself. He had let the team down when they needed him to stay calm and help them. Paul's apologies were accepted by his teammates and his coach.

'Don't worry, you're young,' Deschamps said to him. 'You still have a lot to learn.'

The red card was a good reminder that Paul was still only twenty. With all of the praise flying around him, the sending-off helped him to keep his feet on the ground, just like his mum had always taught him. He was a French international now but he wasn't the complete player yet. As he got older, he would need to get wiser.

CHAPTER 17

GOLDEN BOY

'We're on track for a second league title in a row,'
Andrea said after another Serie A victory.

Paul loved the winning mentality at Juventus.
With Giorgio Chiellini, Andrea Barzagli and
Leonardo Bonucci in defence, they didn't concede
many goals at all. In attack, Andrea's brilliant passes
created goals for Claudio, Arturo, Sebastian, Mirko
Vucinić and Fabio Quagliarella. It was a real team
effort and Paul enjoyed being part of it.

'When I came here, I was hoping to play fifteen
games in my first season,' he told Claudio. 'But I've
played nearly thirty times already and it's only April!'

Manager Antonio Conte had shown great faith

in Paul. Italian football was a difficult place for a youngster – it was a lot more tactical than English football. All of the teams were very well-organised and they made it really hard to be skilful and score goals. Paul had to be patient and clever with the ball. Luckily, he was very determined and a lightning-quick learner. In no time at all, the Juventus fans loved 'Pogboom'.

In the Champions League, Juventus lost to Bayern Munich in the quarter-finals. Paul loved the experience of playing in Europe's biggest club competition but it was disappointing to lose 4-0. As he left the pitch, Gianluigi Buffon put his arm around Paul's shoulder.

'Don't worry, mate,' the veteran keeper said. 'We'll be back next year. Now, it's all about winning the *Italian* league!'

Conte had moved Claudio into the Number 10 role behind the striker, which meant that Paul was playing every game alongside Andrea and Arturo in midfield. It was a big responsibility for a twenty-year-old but Paul was fearless. With such excellent

mentors, his passing was getting better and better
and so was his shooting. Juventus only needed one
point from their match against Palermo to secure
the title.

The atmosphere in the Juventus Stadium was
incredible. The crowd was a sea of black and white
as Paul walked out onto the pitch. Nearly 40,000
fans were there, expecting to see their team win. The
pressure was really on. It was a very tense match but
in the second half, Paul chipped a great pass to Mirko
in the penalty area. The defender barged into him –
penalty! Arturo stepped up and sent the goalkeeper
the wrong way. Juventus had the lead.

'Stay focused!' Gianluigi shouted from his goal as
his teammates celebrated. They were nearly there.

With ten minutes to go, Juventus were still
winning 1-0. As Paul dribbled into the penalty area,
a Palermo defender pushed him in the face. Paul was
furious and his temper got him in trouble again. The
referee showed him a red card and Juventus were
down to ten men.

At the final whistle, the Juventus players hugged

each other but Paul had mixed emotions. On the one hand, he had won his first big trophy but on the other hand, he had let his team down. Players would often try to wind him up and he needed to learn to stay calm.

'For now, enjoy yourself!' Andrea told him as they walked around the pitch, thanking the fans for their support. 'You can think about the sending-off tomorrow.'

Two weeks later, Juventus lifted the Serie A trophy. Paul was the third player to run on to the field and the crowd cheered loudly.

Pogboom! Pogboom! Pogboom!

He gave high-fives to all of the young mascots as he ran past and he waved and clapped to the fans. It felt great to have that heavy, gold medal around his neck. What a first season it had been for Paul. It was beyond his wildest dreams.

The players stood in two lines to form a guard of honour for their manager Conte to walk through. As captain Gianluigi raised the trophy towards the sky, fireworks went off all around the stadium. The players danced and took turns to hold the trophy. It was a very proud and happy day.

Forza Juve! Forza Juve!

There was no summer break for Paul – next up was the FIFA Under-20 World Cup in Turkey. Although he was a full French international now, he was still young enough to qualify and he loved representing his country at any level. Pierre Mankowski, his old coach with the France Under-19s, was in charge again and so there was no doubt about who the captain would be.

'I won't be happy unless we win the whole tournament this time!' Paul told Geoffrey and Samuel as the squad met up to prepare. Paul would wear the Number 6 shirt, just like he did at Juventus.

France were in a group with their big rivals, Spain. When the two teams met, Spain won their match 2-1 but France still finished in second place to qualify for the Round of 16.

'It's not been a good start but we've got the chance to do better!' Paul told his teammates. He was tired after his first long club season but he was ready to give everything to win another trophy.

Against Turkey, Geoffrey scored early on and the game finished 4-1. The French team spirit was great as they celebrated each goal together.

'That's more like it!' Paul said at the final whistle with a big smile on his face.

In the quarterfinal against Uzbekistan, France scored four goals again and this time, Paul scored one from the penalty spot. With a new blond streak through his hair, he coolly stepped up and placed it right in the corner.

At the base of the midfield, Paul protected the defence and started the attacks with his calm, quick passing. Against Ghana in the semi-finals, the score was 1-1 with twenty minutes left. Paul moved forward with the ball and spotted Florian Thauvin's run down the right wing. His pass was perfect and Florian cut inside and fired a low shot into the net.

Goooooooooooooooooooooooaaaaaaaaaaaaaaaaaaaaa aaallllllllllllllllllllllllllllll!!!!!!!!!

Ghana attacked again and again in search of an

equaliser but Paul made lots of tackles and inspired his teammates to keep going until the final whistle.

'We're in the final!' Geoffrey shouted as he hugged Paul.

'Yes but we need to win the final now!' the France captain replied. He was always thinking about the next target.

In the final, even after 120 minutes, it was France 0-0 Uruguay. Paul walked around his teammates as they rested on the grass, patting them on the back and encouraging them.

'We're five good penalties away from winning the World Cup!' he shouted.

Paul took their first and he knew that he would score. There was never any doubt in his mind. When the referee blew the whistle, he slowly trotted towards the ball. The goalkeeper dived to his left but Paul hit it powerfully to the right. As he walked back to the halfway line, he put his hands to his ears to get the crowd going.

Uruguay missed their first two penalties and France scored all four of theirs to win the final. The whole squad celebrated together, jumping up and down in front of the fans.

'What did I say at the start of the tournament?' Paul joked with Samuel. 'I told you we'd go all the way!'

Paul won the Golden Ball as the best player of the tournament, and just when it looked like 2013 couldn't get any better, he won the Golden Boy award too. He was officially the best young player in Europe.

CHAPTER 18

GOALDEN BOY

As Europe's Golden Boy, there was now a lot of pressure on Paul to play brilliantly in every match. He had set himself very high standards and now he had to live up to them consistently. But Paul wasn't worried; he believed in himself and set himself new targets.

'My number one aim is to score more goals this season,' he told his brothers when they went on holiday together. 'In training, my long-range shooting is really good but I need to be more accurate in matches.'

'I scored sixteen for Crewe last season!' Mathias boasted. 'How many did you get?'

'Only five,' Paul admitted. 'But this season I'm aiming for double figures!'

In the Supercoppa Italiana against Lazio, he started on the bench but replaced Claudio who got injured after only twenty minutes. Two minutes later, the ball fell near Paul inside the penalty area. He swivelled his body and sent a left foot shot into the bottom corner. *Booooooooooooooom!*

Gooooooooooooooooooaaaaaaaaaaallllllllllllllllll!!!!!!!!

Paul later set up new signing Carlos Tevez to make it 4-0, and he was named man of the match.

'Is there anything that you haven't won this year?' Carlos joked.

'Yes, the Champions League!' Paul replied immediately.

Despite his ambitions, Juventus really struggled and failed to make it past the group stages. Paul wasn't happy but he focused on another league title instead. Again and again, he was the matchwinner, just when it looked like they were heading for a 0-0 draw. Away to Parma, Juventus were missing chance after chance.

'Keep shooting!' Paul shouted to his teammates. 'Eventually, we'll get the goal we need.'

Fabio's shot hit the crossbar and bounced down in the box. Paul reacted quickly, and with his long legs he got to the ball first and coolly slotted it past the goalkeeper.

'The best players don't just score goals, they score *important* goals' – that was one of his dad's favourite sayings and it was true. Paul's hero Zinedine Zidane did amazing things when his team needed him most. Now, he was doing the same.

Juventus were unstoppable. Against title rivals Napoli a week later, Andrea made it 2-0 with a brilliant free kick.

'Whatever he can do, I can do better!' Paul thought to himself.

He received the ball thirty yards from goal and in plenty of space. Paul's first touch flicked the ball up into the air and so he hit his shot on the volley. *Boooooooooom!* The technique was perfect and the ball flew through the air and straight into the top corner of the net.

Gooooooooooooooooooooaaaaaaaaaaaaaaaalllllllllll llllllllll!!!!!!!!!!

It wasn't just Paul's goals that the fans loved; it was also his style. He changed his hairstyle every week, he posted fun photos and videos on Twitter, and he did cool hip hop dances to celebrate.

Pogboom! Pogboom! Pogboom!

By Christmas, Paul was only one goal behind his total from the previous season. He wasn't afraid to keep shooting, even when he missed lots of shots in a row. Against Sampdoria, he controlled the ball and unleashed a fierce shot into the top corner. It was another wonder strike and he made it look so easy.

Paul lifted up his Juventus shirt to reveal a message for the world: 'R.L.S. CITY BOYS'. It was the name that they had given themselves back in Renardière when they were kids – Paul and his best friends Mamadou, Habib, Nabil and Ounoussou. They were still his best friends. Paul pointed to the words written across his chest. He was very proud of where he was from.

'It's not about *if* we win the title, it's *when*,' Paul

said to Carlos. The Argentinian was having a great first season in Italy and Paul loved playing with such a great goalscorer.

Juventus had won every home game all season but against Bologna, the Italian champions were struggling to score. A win would put them on the verge of reclaiming the Serie A title. Paul was at the centre of everything. He had one shot saved by the goalkeeper and then he put a header over the crossbar. Paul's skills weren't always successful but that never stopped him from trying.

In the second half, Arturo passed to Paul just outside the penalty area. Paul's first touch moved the ball to the right and confused the defenders. He could see a path to goal and so he shot low and hard. The ball skipped over the grass and right into the corner of the net. Paul was the matchwinner yet again.

Goooooooooooooooooaaaaaaaaaaaaaaaaaaaaaaaaallll llllllllllllllllllllllllllll!!!!!!!!!!

'I can't believe you're still only twenty-one!' Andrea said, giving him a big hug.

Paul was showing more maturity now and he had become one of Juventus's most important players. Not only was he a good ball-winner and passer but he was also now a key goalscorer too.

'I want to be the complete midfielder,' he told his teammates. 'A bit of Zizou, a bit of Vieira, a bit of Ronaldinho, a bit of everyone else!'

Paul finished the season with a second league winners' medal. He had played a total of fifty-one matches, more than any other Juventus player. And he had reached his target of ten goals, most of which were amazing strikes.

'You've earned that!' Conte joked with his young player, as they celebrated with the trophy.

But Paul didn't have long to relax and enjoy the success. He was soon off for his next big challenge – World Cup 2014 in Brazil.

CHAPTER 19

WORLD CUP 2014

'Hi all! We are the Pog family. We will manage Paul's account until the end of the World Cup!'

Paul had lots of Twitter followers and so, while he was away in Brazil, he left his mum ('Mamso') and brothers ('Le Dos' and 'Ya'Flo') in charge of keeping them updated. They posted a cool cartoon of all four of them.

Paul was one of the youngest members of the France squad but that didn't matter. His power and skill would be crucial for linking the midfield with Antoine Griezmann and Karim Benzema in attack.

'We need you running box to box,' Patrice told him. 'I'm getting old now but you've got long, fresh legs!'

The atmosphere in Brazil was crazy. The streets

were full of noise and colour as football took over the country. It was like a month-long carnival. Paul enjoyed watching the people dancing and playing beach football. It wasn't party time for him, however – he was focused on doing his best for his country.

France weren't one of the main favourites to win the tournament but the nation hoped that their team could at least get to the semi-finals, even without their star playmaker Franck Ribéry. Paul was full of confidence, especially with legends Zidane and Vieira there to offer advice.

'We're the dark horses!' he told Patrice. 'Everyone's talking about Germany, Spain and Brazil but we're good enough to beat them all.'

Meanwhile, the Pog Family got ready for the tournament with a video of all three brothers doing the 'The Pogdance'. People loved their fun spirit.

In the first match against Honduras, Yohan Cabaye floated a free kick into the penalty. With his height, Paul was always a threat from set pieces. He chested the ball down beautifully but an opponent pushed him to the floor. Penalty! Karim scored the penalty and the match finished 3-0.

'That's a great start!' captain Hugo Lloris said in the dressing room afterwards.

On Twitter, Mamso, Le Dos and Ya'Flo celebrated every goal, and back in Roissy-en-Brie, everyone cheered on their local hero. Paul was a substitute for the second match against Switzerland but he came on with half an hour to go. France were already winning 3-0 but Paul was desperate to impress and reclaim his starting role. A few minutes after coming on, the ball came to him on the right.

Two seasons of playing with Andrea had taught him a lot about reading the game. When Karim made a great run behind the defence, Paul played an amazing pass with the outside of his right foot. The defender tried to block it but he could only deflect it into Karim's path, who tapped it past the goalkeeper to make it 4-0.

'What a top-quality pass!' Karim said as they hugged.

France were through to the second round and everything was going according to plan. Paul's brilliant assist against Switzerland won him a starting spot alongside Yohan and Blaise Matuidi in midfield. The Pog Family posted a cartoon of 'Paulverine', ready for battle with long metal claws like the *X-Men* comic-book character, Wolverine.

'It's knock-out football now,' Hugo reminded the team before kick-off against Nigeria. 'It's going to be a very tight match so we need to take our chances!'

With ten minutes left, the score was 0-0. Paul thought his manager Didier Deschamps might replace him with a striker – but he was still on the pitch, and it was time to show why.

Mathieu Valbuena's corner came to Paul at the back post. He used his strong neck muscles to head the ball over the defenders and into the back of the net.

Goooooooooooooooooooooooooooaaaaaaaaaaaaaaaaa aalllllllllllllllllllllllllllllllll!!!!!!!!!!!

Paul's teammates jumped on him. Yet again, he had scored at a really important time.

'That's world-class,' Patrice told him. His teammate's praise meant a lot to Paul.

'I'm proud of my son!' 'Mamso' tweeted with a

picture of Paul holding the man of the match trophy.

In the quarter-finals, France were up against one of the favourites, Germany.

'They're a great side but Ghana and Algeria have both tested them,' Deschamps told his players. 'If we play as well as we have so far, we can definitely win this.'

Paul couldn't wait for the big match. The team was getting better every time they played together. There was a good balance between hard-working players like Blaise and Yohan, and skilful attackers like Antoine and Mathieu. Paul was a winning combination of the two styles.

Rio de Janeiro's huge Maracanã Stadium was full of fans in white or blue. It was a really hot day and Paul could feel the sweat on his forehead as the French national anthem played. He sang along with his eyes closed, picturing the game ahead and what he would do.

'Come on!' Hugo shouted, clapping his big goalkeeper gloves loudly.

An early goal from Germany was a killer blow. It

wasn't Paul's best performance but he tried his best to drive his team forward with his dribbling. They had several chances to equalise but thanks to some great goalkeeping from Manuel Neuer, the match finished 1-0.

As the German players celebrated, the French players wandered around the pitch in shock. Antoine and Mathieu were in tears.

'We made one mistake all game!' Paul complained to Patrice. He was devastated.

'I know, it's just not fair,' Patrice replied. It would be his last World Cup. 'You'll just have to get revenge for us in 2018.'

It had been a great first international tournament for Paul, even if he hadn't quite achieved what he wanted. After the final, he was named as the World Cup's Best Young Player. It was yet another prize to add to his growing collection.

'I'm back,' Paul tweeted a few days later. 'Almost one million followers! Thanks #ThePogFamily!'

CHAPTER 20

CHALLENGING FOR THE CHAMPIONS LEAGUE AGAIN

'Welcome, Tonton Pat!' After a return to Renardière and a holiday in New York City, Paul was back in Turin to meet an old friend. He had a nickname for everyone.

'Thanks, mate,' Patrice said with a big smile on his face. 'I really missed you in Manchester, so I thought I'd join you at Juventus!'

It was great to have another friend at the club, and soon he had family living in Italy too.

'I've signed for Pescara!' Mathias told him excitedly on the phone. The club played in Serie B and Paul was really pleased for his brother. 'Le Dos' would now only be a five-hour drive away.

With Paul's reputation growing all the time, other big European clubs were interested in signing him for a lot of money. It was nice to be linked with Barcelona and Real Madrid but Paul wasn't ready to leave Juventus.

'We've got a really good squad here and we can challenge for the Champions League this year,' he told his agent, Mino. 'Why would I go now?'

Instead, Paul signed a big new contract and prepared for the season ahead. He couldn't wait to compete for the treble – Serie A, the Coppa Italia and, most importantly, the Champions League.

But disappointing defeats at Atlético Madrid and Olympiakos left Juventus in a difficult position in Europe. They needed to win at least two of their last three games to qualify for the next round.

'We can do so much better than this!' Paul said to Carlos before their return match against Olympiakos.

An amazing Andrea free kick put Juventus in front but the Greek team equalised and then took the lead.

An own goal made it 2-2 but a draw wasn't enough. The fans in the Juventus Stadium urged their team to get a winner.

Forza Juve! Forza Juve!

The ball came to Paul just inside the penalty area. He had his back to goal and so he tried a cheeky flick to Carlos. The defender blocked the pass but the ball came back to Paul. This time, he was facing the goal and his shot flew into the bottom corner.

Boooooooooom!

Goooooooooooooooaaaaaaaaaaaaallllllllllllll llll!!!!!!!!

The crowd went wild. His teammates tried to hug him but Paul dodged them all and ran towards the bench. This was his most important goal yet – their Champions League dream was still alive! Paul jumped up into the air with his fist pumped. He loved being the hero.

In the second round, Juventus beat Borussia Dortmund 5-1 on aggregate. Carlos scored three and Paul got two key assists.

'We can do this!' Gianluigi shouted as they

celebrated the victory. The feeling of team spirit was excellent.

Paul missed the quarter-final against Monaco because of a hamstring injury but Juventus won 1-0 thanks to an Arturo penalty. Next, they faced giants Real Madrid in the semi-finals.

'I have to be fit for those games!' Paul told the club physio.

He worked really hard in the gym but it wasn't quite enough. Paul had to watch from the stands as Juventus won the first leg 2-1.

'Well played, guys!' he told his teammates in the dressing room afterwards. 'I hated watching but it was a great performance. Don't worry; I'll be back for the second leg!'

At Real Madrid's Bernabéu stadium, Juventus just needed to avoid defeat to make the final but that was a very difficult task. Cristiano Ronaldo, Gareth Bale and Karim Benzema scored goals for fun. Paul knew that he had to be at his best, both in defence and in attack.

Gianluigi made save after save but halfway

through the first half, the referee awarded Real Madrid a penalty. Ronaldo scored to make it 1-0. Juventus needed to score, or they would be out of the Champions League.

'Don't panic,' manager Massimiliano Allegri told his team at half-time. 'If we all attack, Madrid will score again and this game will be over. We have forty-five minutes to get a goal.'

Paul tried to get forward as much as possible. Andrea's free kick was headed away but Paul stayed in the penalty area. Arturo's ball back into the box was perfect. Defender Sergio Ramos sprinted over to challenge him but Paul used his height to win the header. Not only that, but he headed it straight to striker Álvaro Morata. He chested the ball down and shot past the keeper Iker Casillas.

Goooooooooooooooooooooaaaaaaaaaaaaaaaaaaaaaa llllllllllllllllllllllllllll!!!!!!!!!!!!!!!!!!!

'What an assist!' Andrea shouted, giving Paul a big hug.

The last half an hour was very tense but Juventus held on. At the final whistle, they celebrated together in front of their fans. It was the best feeling of Paul's life.

'Now we just need to beat Barcelona!' he said to Patrice.

Juventus went into the Champions League final full of confidence. They had won the Serie A title again and the Coppa Italia too. The double was great but the treble would be amazing. Barcelona were also going for the treble.

'Messi, Suarez and Neymar have scored over a hundred goals between them this season!' Carlos said on the flight to Berlin.

'I know but we're a real team and we work hard together,' Paul replied. As ever, he wanted to be really positive about the match. They needed to be fearless.

Paul had dreamed about playing in a Champions League final since he was five years old. As he walked out of the tunnel and onto the pitch, he walked past the huge silver trophy. He had never wanted to win anything so much. With the famous tournament anthem playing through the stadium, Paul got goosebumps. He had come so far and he was still only twenty-two years old. This was the biggest stage and Paul was desperate to shine on it.

Barcelona took the lead after just four minutes but Juventus didn't give up. Paul ran forward down the left and his cross was nearly inch-perfect for Carlos but Barcelona managed to clear. Then early in the second half, Álvaro scored an equaliser.

'Game on!' Carlos shouted. 'We need to get a second goal quickly.'

Paul ran and ran but he wasn't quite at his powerful best. When he got the ball in front of goal, he shot straight at the keeper. Paul was playing as a third striker. Arturo crossed from the right and Paul controlled it beautifully but Dani Alves wrestled him to the floor.

'Penalty!' Paul screamed but the referee said no. He couldn't believe it.

As Juve attacked and attacked, Barcelona counter-attacked and Suárez made it 2-1. Paul kept going but his header flew over the bar. It just wasn't his day. In the last minute, Neymar scored to secure the victory.

It was a tough defeat to take but Juventus had done everything that they could against a brilliant team. As Paul left the pitch, he felt frustrated but proud. He would have plenty more opportunities to win Europe's top competition.

CHAPTER 21

THE DAB

Paul loved the USA. He often went there on holiday because it was the home of his two favourite things other than football: basketball and rap music. Michael Jordan was one of his biggest basketball heroes and he had been listening to hip-hop music since his days in Renardière with the R.L.S. City Boys. As he became more and more famous, Paul made friends with lots of NBA players and rap stars. He posted photos with them on his Instagram account, as well as videos of him dancing and shooting hoops.

When he returned to Juventus for the 2015–16 season, Paul was now the club's superstar. Andrea had gone to play in America, Carlos had returned to

Argentina and Arturo had moved to Bayern Munich. There was a lot of pressure on Paul but he was ready to step up and take on even more responsibility. He wore the Number 10 shirt now, and he had a brilliant new goal celebration to show off.

'Check out this new dance craze!' Paul said to his new teammate Paulo Dybala as they sat together on the team bus.

In the rap music video the pair were watching, the dancer dropped his head down onto his arm and then raised his arm and elbow up into the air.

'It's called "The Dab",' Paul explained.

'It looks like he's sneezing!' Paulo responded.

It did look strange at first but his Instagram fans loved it. Paul couldn't wait to show off the new Pogdance when he scored. It was all part of his stylish image. His haircuts were getting more and more interesting – first he shaved a star into the side of his head, then zebra stripes and then leopard spots.

'I'm definitely your son, Mamso!' Paul joked to Yeo. 'You're always changing your hairstyle and so am I!'

After a slow start to the season, Juventus were back in great form by Christmas. Paul was the main man in midfield alongside Claudio and German midfielder Sami Khedira. Against Carpi, Claudio had the ball in his own half when he saw Paul's great forward run. His long pass was incredible and suddenly Paul was through on goal. He chested the ball down and as the keeper came out to block the shot, he placed it past him and into the net.

Gooooooooooooooooooooooooooaaaaaaaaaaaaaaaaa aaaaaaaaalllllllllllllllllllllll!!!!!!!

Paul fell over as he scored but he got up straight away and ran towards the fans. It was time for 'The Dab'. He dropped his head onto one arm and raised it towards the sky and then did the same with the other arm. It looked a bit like a bow and Paul added some more dance steps too.

After that, he did it every time he scored and soon Paulo was doing it too.

'They're calling us the Dab Brothers!' Paul laughed. The young stars were forming a great partnership in attack.

It wasn't long before other footballers were also doing 'The Dab'. Jesse Lingard, Paul's friend from his days at Manchester United, loved it and brought it to the Premier League. Everton striker Romelu Lukaku, another of Paul's football friends, joined in as well. Even if he wasn't playing in England, Paul was still having a big impact there.

'What can I say, I'm a trendsetter!' he joked with Jesse on the phone.

Paul wasn't interested in being a boring, quiet player. He wanted to be a superstar with lots of personality and style. In January 2016, Paul was picked for the FIFA World Team of the Year alongside Messi, Ronaldo and Neymar. It was a massive honour for him and he was invited to a fancy ceremony in Switzerland. The other players brought their wives or girlfriends, but Paul had other ideas.

'Mamso, you're coming to the ceremony with me!' he told his mum on the phone.

They had a great time walking the red carpet together, especially as Paul had chosen a flashy outfit for the night. While the other players wore smart black suits, he wore a black velvet jacket covered in gold flowers, and sported a trendy pair of glasses. He was the talk of the town and he loved it.

'Come and do "The Dab" with me!' he said to the legendary Dutch player Edgar Davids. 'That one's for Instagram!'

Paul loved entertaining his fans but he never stopped working hard. He posted videos of his tough fitness workouts and he was always one of the last players to leave the training ground each day.

Back on the pitch, Napoli and Roma were both challenging for the title but Juventus were too strong. Away at AC Milan, they were drawing 1-1. One point wasn't enough, however. They needed all three. They took shot after shot and Paul hit the post with an amazing free kick.

'We're getting close,' he told Sami. 'Don't worry, we'll get a winner.'

Claudio's corner went deep to the back post and Paul chested it down brilliantly. There were defenders all around him but his long leg stretched towards the ball and guided it into the net. There was no 'Dab' this time. He was just delighted to have scored such a vital goal.

'We're on for a fourth Serie A title in a row!' Paul said at the final whistle.

He was playing in a more attacking, creative role now and he really enjoyed having more time on the ball. With his pace and power, he ran from box to box all game long. He could do everything and that made him really difficult to play against. Paul scored eight league goals and, more importantly, he finished the season with twelve assists. He was the best playmaker in Italy.

Despite losing three of their key players at the start of the 2015–16 season, Juventus still won the league and cup double again. Paul was their key player but he wasn't satisfied.

'I've still got lots to learn,' he told Mino at the end of the season. 'I'm determined to be the best and I'm not the best yet.'

'You're only twenty-three!' his agent replied but Paul didn't listen. There was no end to his ambition.

CHAPTER 22

EURO 2016

'The pressure is on but we've got to win this!' Paul said to Patrice as they joined up with the national team to prepare for Euro 2016.

With the tournament taking place on home soil, France were the favourites. They had brilliant young talents like Paul and Antoine Griezmann, more experienced stars like Patrice and Olivier Giroud, and on-form players like West Ham's Dimitri Payet. It was a great recipe for success.

'Yes, the country is relying on us to bring some joy,' Patrice replied.

The opening match against Romania was really tough. France played well but their opponents defended strongly. At half-time, it was still 0-0 but Paul knew all about being patient.

'We'll get the goal eventually!' he told his teammates in the dressing room.

Paul was right. Olivier headed Dimitri's cross into the back of the net and the Stade de France crowd went wild. There were French flags waving everywhere. It meant so much to the nation. Paul was the first to jump on Olivier and soon the whole team was hugging.

Only a few minutes later, however, Romania equalised from the penalty spot. France were heading for a disappointing draw, but Dimitri wasn't finished yet. His amazing shot from the edge of the box flew into the top corner. It had been a really dramatic finale but *Les Bleus* had the three points they wanted.

'We needed to start with a victory and we got it,' captain Hugo Lloris said at the final whistle. There was a strong squad spirit. 'But we have to do much better in our next match.'

Paul was disappointed with his own performance.

His passing was good and he nearly scored
with a volley but there was plenty of room for
improvement. With players like Anthony Martial and
Moussa Sissoko on the bench, Paul needed to be at
his box-to-box best.

'This is my time to shine,' he said to Antoine
Griezmann. 'I need to show the world that I can do
great things at the highest level, just like Vieira and
Zidane.'

'Me too but we're a real team,' his teammate
replied. 'If we don't have our shooting boots on,
Olivier and Dimitri step up instead!'

Paul was on the bench for the second game against
Albania but he came on at half-time. His attacking
runs got the team moving forward but again, France
were on the verge of a draw. They needed a goal and
this time Antoine was the hero with a well-placed
header.

Then in the last minute, Paul got the ball in
his own half. He looked up and spotted Olivier's
movement towards the left wing. He slipped as he
kicked it, but Paul's long pass was absolutely perfect.

Olivier ran towards goal and Dimitri finished off the counter-attack with a great shot.

'That pass was Pirlo-esque!' Olivier shouted over the noise of the French fans celebrating.

Paul loved being compared to one of his heroes. He had worked hard to learn from Andrea and it was nice to see it really paying off.

In the second round, France were up against the Republic of Ireland and there was a very early shock. As Paul chased Shane Long into the box, one of his long legs clipped the striker's leg. Long fell to the floor. Penalty! France were 1-0 down and it was Paul's fault.

'Don't worry,' Patrice said, putting his arm around Paul's shoulder. 'We've got a long time left to score!'

Paul did his best to make up for his mistake. He set up lots of attacks and his long-range free kick came very close to going into the top corner. In the second half, Antoine scored an amazing header to make it 1-1.

'Thanks!' Paul said as they celebrated. 'Now, let's go and win this.'

Three minutes later, centre-back Adil Rami played a long ball up to Olivier and he headed it down beautifully into Antoine's path. He dribbled towards goal and calmly slotted the ball past the goalkeeper. Antoine had a celebratory dance of his own to display although it wasn't as cool as 'The Dab'.

'That's just embarrassing!' Paul joked.

Paul was really pleased that Antoine was playing so well but he wanted to be one of France's stars too. In the quarter-final match against Iceland, he would need to do better.

Olivier made it 1-0 and then from Antoine's corner, Paul jumped high and put a powerful header into the top corner.

Goooooooooooooooooooooooaaaaaaaaaaaaaaaaaaa aaaaaaaalllllllllllllllllllll!!!!!!!!!!!

It was such a relief for Paul to finally get himself on the scoresheet in the tournament, and a great way to get his confidence back. France were unstoppable as Dimitri and Antoine made it 4-0 by half-time. The game finished 5-2 – and they were through to the semi-finals.

'What a performance!' Hugo cheered. 'The timing is perfect. We'll need to play just as well against Germany.'

They carried on their good form and just before half-time, they were awarded a penalty for a handball. Antoine stepped up and sent the goalkeeper the wrong way. 1-0! The Stade Vélodrome in Marseille was bouncing. France were just forty-five minutes away from the final.

'We need to stay organised and defend well,' manager Didier Deschamps told his players. 'But let's try to get a second goal if we can.'

Germany tried to pass the ball out from defence but France didn't let them. Paul worked hard to steal the ball on the left side of the penalty area. Olivier was in the box, calling for the cross, and Paul was one-on-one with the left-back. It was time to show off his skills. After two step-overs with his right foot, he tricked the defender and dragged the ball onto his left foot. Paul's cross was going straight on to Olivier's head but goalkeeper Manuel Neuer came out to clear. The ball fell to Antoine and he poked it into the net. 2-0! France were heading to the final and Paul had played a key role.

'That skill was magical!' Antoine said after the game. He was glad to see the old Paul back – and just in time for the biggest match of all.

After losing the Champions League final in 2015, Paul was desperate to win a major tournament. But Portugal, with a team including Ronaldo, Nani and the new young star Renato Sanches, were very difficult opponents. When Ronaldo got injured in the first half, Portugal didn't suffer. Indeed, they looked even more determined to win. For the first time all tournament, Paul, Antoine, Dimitri and Olivier all struggled in attack. After ninety minutes, it was still 0-0.

'We need a moment of genius,' Deschamps told his tired team. 'We don't want this to go to penalties.'

Paul ran and ran but he couldn't create a match-winning moment. After 110 minutes, the Portuguese substitute Éder hit a wonder strike from twenty-five yards. It flew past Hugo and into the bottom corner.

For France, the dream was over – at least until World
Cup 2018.

As he walked off the pitch at the final whistle, Paul
was devastated. It hadn't been his best tournament
but there had been great moments. That first
international winner's medal he longed for would
just have to wait.

CHAPTER 23

REUNITED

'José Mourinho wants you back at Old Trafford!'
Mino told Paul.

As Paul relaxed in the USA after the disappointment
of the Euros, this was massive news. It made him
think long and hard about his club career. After four
great seasons at Juventus, was it time for a new
challenge? He had won everything in Italy.

'I want to win the Champions League,' Paul said
to his mum, 'and I'm not sure that I can do that
here.'

'But can you do that at Manchester United?' Yeo
replied. European giants Real Madrid were also
interested in signing him and their manager was

Paul's hero Zinedine Zidane. Zizou had already called him 'a complete player', which was the best compliment ever.

'And do you want to go back to Manchester United?' Yeo continued. 'I always thought it was your destiny to return but you need to be sure that it's what you want.'

Despite the controversial transfer to Juventus, Paul had very fond memories of his time at Manchester United four years earlier. He still had lots of friends there, like Jesse and Adnan, and it really felt like home.

'If they had believed in me more back then, I would never have left,' Paul told his mum.

He had unfinished business in England. Manchester United weren't in the Champions League but with Mourinho in charge, the club could become great again. The manager had big plans and lots of money to spend on new signings.

'I'm building a great team for the future,' Mourinho told Paul, 'and I want you to be my superstar at the centre of it.'

It was a very tempting offer. In attack, they had Wayne Rooney and young stars Marcus Rashford and Anthony Martial but what United desperately needed was a midfield playmaker. Paul would have the freedom to control the game and make his great attacking runs.

'I'll make you the best midfielder in the world. You can be the heart of Manchester United for the next decade,' Mourinho added.

Paul loved the United manager's positive attitude and he wasn't the only one trying to persuade him to return. Jesse was sending him many text messages and while he was in Los Angeles, Paul met up with Zlatan Ibrahimović for dinner. Paul had lots of respect for the Swedish striker and they shared the same agent.

'I'm going to Manchester United and you're coming with me!' Zlatan told him with a big smile. 'Together, we'll take the Premier League by storm. You'll love José Mourinho – he's the perfect manager for you. I've told Mino that Old Trafford is the only place for you.'

The transfer rumours continued all summer. Everyone was talking about it. Manchester United legends Ryan Giggs, Paul Scholes and Rio Ferdinand all said that Paul would be a great signing for the club. On Twitter, the hashtag '#POGBACK' was really popular.

'We hope to make one more signing this summer,' Mourinho said at a press conference. The Manchester United fans all crossed their fingers that it would be 'Ferguson's biggest mistake', as they liked to call him.

Paul's mind was made up but the negotiations took much longer than he expected. How much money did Juventus want and how much were Manchester United prepared to pay for him?

'What's taking so long?' Paul asked Mino. He couldn't wait to get started.

'Be patient, we're nearly there,' his agent told him.

Finally, in early August 2016, the transfer was completed. A superstar signing needed a superstar announcement, so MUTV posted a Hollywood-style video. Paul stood in the darkness with his hood up and slowly the camera zoomed in as he pulled down his hood to reveal a new haircut: the club badge shaved into the side of his dyed blonde hair. 'I'm back!' Paul said. 'REUNITED' was the clever slogan they used.

Paul sent messages to the Juventus fans through social media: 'The club will always be a part of me and I will always miss, love and be grateful to the club, the team and especially the supporters.'

It was hard to say goodbye to his Italian home but it was time to go back to his English home.

'This is the place for me to achieve everything that I want to achieve,' Paul told the media as he posed in the new Manchester United shirt with his favourite 'Number 6' on his back.

The fee of £89 million made Paul the most expensive player in the world. It put a lot of pressure on him but he tried to ignore it. He focused on getting back on the pitch and giving his all to help his club to win trophies again.

'Welcome back!' Jesse said, giving him a big hug, when he arrived at training. 'Manchester City,

Chelsea and Arsenal better watch out!'

Paul made his big return at Old Trafford against Southampton. As he walked out of the tunnel, the Manchester United fans were all on their feet, cheering his name. Paul was everywhere – dribbling, passing, tackling, shooting. With him in the team, United suddenly had a lot more energy. The supporters loved the excitement that he brought to football.

When Wayne crossed into the box, Paul jumped for the header but he couldn't quite reach it. Luckily, Zlatan was behind him to head it into the net.

'This is just the start!' Zlatan said as they celebrated the goal together.

A few weeks later, when Paul scored his first United goal, in a 4-1 victory over Leicester City, it was one of his proudest ever moments. He was so happy to be back. It had been a remarkable journey from France to England to Italy and then back to England. He had left Manchester as a promising youngster and he had returned four years later as one of the best players in the world. He still had a lot to prove in the Premier League but Paul was looking forward to the challenge.

With his winning combination of power, ambition, style and skill, the boy from Renardière was unstoppable.

Turn the page for a special bonus
chapter of Paul Pogba's journey to
the World Cup. . .

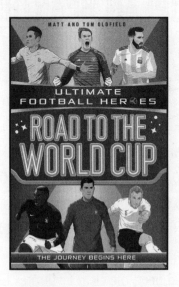

Chapter taken from *Road to the World Cup*
by Matt and Tom Oldfield

Available now!

PART ONE

EUROPEAN HEARTBREAK

Stade de France, 10 July 2016

The Euro 2016 final was over – France 0 Portugal 1. As Cristiano Ronaldo went wild with his teammates, Paul stood there on the pitch, alone and in shock. Had that really just happened?

France had been the clear favourites to win. Their team was playing brilliantly. Captain Hugo Lloris was making amazing saves in goal, Paul was playing awesome passes in midfield and Antoine Griezmann was on fire in attack. They had beaten World Champions Germany in the semi-final, and they were playing on home soil. What could go wrong?

The Stade de France was covered in the national

colours – blue, white and red. The atmosphere was incredible until the 109th minute. That's when Eder scored the goal that broke French hearts. With the whole country expecting victory, their dream final had turned into a nightmare. Cristiano had gone off injured early on, and they still couldn't score against Portugal.

'How did we lose that?' Paul asked himself. He lifted his shirt over his face to hide his tears.

After a few minutes, his teammate Patrice Evra came over and put an arm around his shoulder. 'Hey, we did our best out there. It just wasn't our night. You'll be back and next time, you'll win!'

Paul always listened to his 'Uncle Pat'. They had known each other for years, ever since Paul was the star of the Manchester United youth team and Patrice was the first-team left-back. Whenever Paul had a bad game or missed home, 'Uncle Pat' was always there to help and offer advice. But at the age of thirty-five, this would be Patrice's last international tournament.

'I know, but I wanted to win the Euros with

you, and I wanted to win it *here*,' Paul muttered, looking up into the stands above them. Most of the disappointed French fans had already gone home.

The Stade de France was where Paul's childhood hero, Zinedine Zidane, had won the 1998 World Cup for his country. Thanks to his two amazing headers, France had beaten Ronaldo's Brazil. Paul still remembered watching the final on TV in Renardière with his brothers, aged five. Eighteen years later, he had hoped to be his country's hero against the other Ronaldo, Portugal's Cristiano.

'Next time,' Paul told himself.

He wanted to escape straight down the tunnel, but instead he did the right thing and stayed on the pitch. To be a great winner, he had to be a great loser too. Paul shook hands with all the Portugal players. He went up on the stage to collect his silver runners-up medal, but it didn't stay around his neck for long.

'Gold is the only medal that I'm interested in,' he told Anthony Martial as they walked away.

Back in the silent dressing room, Antoine looked

even more upset than Paul. He had missed a few good chances in the final and he blamed himself.

'No man, this is a team!' Paul said, hugging his friend. 'We win together, and we lose together.'

Once all the players were sitting down, their manager Didier Deschamps spoke to them.

'Right now, you're disappointed, devastated. I understand. You've worked really hard and I'm proud of you all. But in a couple of months, our next challenge begins. Let's learn our lessons from tonight and go and win the 2018 World Cup!'

In fact, their Road to the World Cup began even earlier than that. Just two weeks after the Euro 2016 final, the qualification group draw took place in Russia. France would be playing in Group A against...

Netherlands...

Sweden...

Bulgaria...

Belarus...

and Luxembourg.

The top team in each group would qualify

automatically for the World Cup and the runner-up would go into the play-offs.

'I'm happy with that draw,' Paul told Antoine when they saw France's opponents. 'There's no-one we can't beat. Russia here we come!'

Juventus

🏆 Serie A: 2012–13, 2013–14, 2014–15, 2015–16

🏆 Supercoppa Italiana: 2013, 2015

🏆 Coppa Italia: 2014–15, 2015–16

🏆 UEFA Champions League Runners-up: 2014–15

France

🏆 FIFA U-20 World Cup: 2013

🏆 UEFA European Championship Runners-up: 2016

Individual

🏆 FIFA U-20 World Cup Golden Ball: 2013

🏆 Golden Boy: 2013

🏆 FIFA World Cup Best Young Player: 2014

🏆 UEFA Team of the Year: 2015

🏆 FIFA FIFPro World XI: 2015

POGBA

6 THE FACTS

NAME:
Paul Labile Pogba

DATE OF BIRTH:
15 March 1993

AGE: 25

PLACE OF BIRTH:
Roissy-en-Brie

NATIONALITY: France

BEST FRIEND: His mother, 'Mamso'

CURRENT CLUB: Manchester United

POSITION: CM

THE STATS

Height (cm):	**191**
Club appearances:	**236**
Club goals:	**43**
Club trophies:	**10**
International appearances:	**51**
International goals:	**9**
International trophies:	**0**
Ballon d'Ors:	**0**

★ ★ ★ **HERO RATING: 87** ★ ★ ★

GREATEST MOMENTS

Type and search the web links to see the magic for yourself!

1 **10TH APRIL 2011,**
CHELSEA 3-2 MANCHESTER UNITED

https://www.youtube.com/watch?v=UnYsbNLd8d8

Manchester United lost the first leg of this FA Youth Cup semi-final, but Paul's powerful late header from Jesse Lingard's cross gave them hope for the second leg. United won that 4-0 and then beat Sheffield United in the final. Paul and Jesse were stars in the making.

★ 2 20TH OCTOBER 2012, JUVENTUS 2-0 NAPOLI

https://www.youtube.com/watch?v=VPyKAqETH8k
After his big move from England to Italy, Paul started playing regular first-team football. He scored his first Juventus goal in Serie A against Napoli and what a goal it was. His left-foot volley flew into the bottom corner from 25 yards out. Suddenly, leaving Manchester United looked like the best decision Paul had ever made.

★ 3 13TH JULY 2013, FRANCE 0-0 URUGUAY (4-1 ON PENALTIES)

https://www.youtube.com/watch?v=209JjGOdW9c
Paul was France's captain at the 2013 FIFA Under-20 World Cup in Turkey. From central midfield, he led his team to glory. In the final against Uruguay, Paul stayed calm and scored his team's first penalty in the shoot-out. As well as lifting the trophy, he also won the Golden Ball as the tournament's best player.

30TH JUNE 2014, FRANCE 2-0 NIGERIA

https://www.youtube.com/watch?v=hm5coliOhZc

The 2014 World Cup in Brazil was Paul's first big senior international tournament. In France's Round of 16 tie against Nigeria, it was 0-0 with 15 minutes to go. A corner fell to Paul at the back-post and he steered his header cleverly into the net. France were through to the quarter-finals and Paul was their hero.

24TH SEPTEMBER 2016, MANCHESTER UNITED 4-1 LEICESTER

https://www.youtube.com/watch?v=Xdhc8VD5SQ4

After his £89million return to Old Trafford, Paul was under a lot of pressure to succeed. Against Premier League champions Leicester City, he ran the show from midfield. After helping to create the first three goals, he scored the fourth himself with a header from a corner. It was his first ever goal for United.

PLAY LIKE YOUR HEROES

HIT LONG-RANGE STRIKES LIKE POGBOOM

SEE IT HERE YouTube

https://www.youtube.com/watch?v=cmLMRuD7Mlc

STEP 1: Move forward from midfield, looking for your goalscoring chance.

STEP 2: If the ball comes to you on the floor, take one touch to control it and move it into a shooting position.

STEP 3: Then strike the ball as quickly as you can, before the defenders and goalkeeper are ready.

STEP 4: Put maximum power, swerve and dip on your shot by hitting it hard, with the laces. That way, the keeper has no chance of saving it as the ball flies into the top corner.

STEP 5: If the ball comes to you in the air, no problem. Don't take a touch; just hit it first time on the volley.

TEST YOUR KNOWLEDGE

QUESTIONS

1. What nicknames do the members of 'The PogFamily' have when Paul is growing up?

2. Which player became Paul's hero after the 1998 World Cup?

3. Who was Paul's favourite player in the French League between 2001 and 2003?

4. How many clubs did Paul play for in France?

5. How old was Paul when he moved to Manchester United?

MATT AND TOM OLDFIELD

6. Which other current Manchester United player was in the youth team with Paul from 2009-11?

7. Which footballer played alongside Paul for Manchester United, Juventus and France?

8. Name the two superstar central midfielders that Paul learned lots from training with.

9. Paul was sent off on his senior debut for France – true or false?

10. Who was Paul's Dab Brother at Juventus?

11. How many different numbers has Paul worn for Manchester United and Juventus?

Answers below. . . No cheating!

1. *Their mum is called 'Mamso', Mathias is 'Le Dos', Florentin is 'Le Zerr' and Paul is 'La Pioche'.* **2.** *Zinedine Zidane* **3.** *Ronaldinho.* **4.** *Three – US Roissy, US Torcy and Le Havre.* **5.** *16.* **6.** *Jesse Lingard.* **7.** *Patrice Evra.* **8.** *Paul Scholes at Manchester United and Andrea Pirlo at Juventus.* **9.** *False – he got a red card in his 2nd match, against Spain.* **10.** *Paulo Dybala.* **11.** *Three – 42 at Manchester United, 10 at Juventus, and 6 for both Juventus and Manchester United .*

This summer, your favourite football heroes will pull on their country's colours to go head-to-head for the ultimate prize – the World Cup.

Celebrate by making sure you have six of the best Ultimate Football Heroes, now with limited-edition international covers!

☆ COMING 31ST MAY ☆